# A VILLAGE AT WAR

## White Waltham 1939-45

This edition dedicated
to the memory of Bert Goodchild

DENNIS TOMLINSON

Ameliel Press

A VILLAGE AT WAR

First published 1998 by

Ameliel Press
66 Greenborough Road
Sprowston
Norwich NR7 9HJ

2nd Edition 1999
3rd Edition 2002

ISBN 0 953 4505 46 - 4th revised edition

Copyright © Dennis Tomlinson 2005

Typeset & Printed by
CATTON PRINT of NORWICH

# A VILLAGE AT WAR

## WHITE WALTHAM 1939-45

## CONTENTS

ACKNOWLEDGMENTS
CHAPTER 1 How it All Started
CHAPTER 2 "We're Building an Airfield"
CHAPTER 3 The Home Guard on Patrol
CHAPTER 4 School Days and the Flying Blackboard
CHAPTER 5 Jobs for the Girls at Anti-Attrition
CHAPTER 6 ML Aviation's War-time Role
CHAPTER 7 One of Ours or One of Theirs?
CHAPTER 8 Keeping the Planes Flying
CHAPTER 9 Paley Street Carries on
CHAPTER 10 Woodlands Park Takes Shelter
CHAPTER 11 The RAF Moves In
CHAPTER 12 All Set for D-Day
CHAPTER 13 Past and Present
List of books on Air Transport Auxiliary
Appendix I: Spitfire Ia - "The Best Thing I Ever Flew"
Appendix II: 'I Only Want You To Do Ten Minutes'
Appendix III: Life As A Ferry Pilot For The RAF
Appendix IV: A Pilot to Remember
Appendix V: We Never Fired in Anger

COVER PHOTOGRAPH:
*Bert Goodchild, the White Waltham schoolboy who achieved his ambition of flying a Spitfire. He is pictured in the cockpit of a Spitfire Mk IX, in 1978.*

# ACKNOWLEDGMENTS

Many people have helped in the preparation of this book. I would like to thank particularly those who have delved into their memories to provide war-time reminiscences and into desks and drawers to find photographs. I would also like to thank the following organisations who have all helped fill in pieces of this jigsaw of history:

>The Public Record Office, Norfolk County Library,
>Berkshire Record Office, Maidenhead Public Library,
>Air Transport Auxiliary Association,
>Museum of Berkshire Aviation.

I would also like to thank my wife for her patience, for taking many telephone calls and for reading through the manuscript and making a number of valuable suggestions.

Further help for the third edition came from Richard Poad, chairman of Maidenhead Heritage Trust, and this is gladly acknowledged. Every effort has been made to trace copyright owners of material contained in this book. If any copyrightholder has not been acknowledged, then this would be corrected in any subsequent edition.

For this fourth edition, I am particularly indebted to Roger Goodchild, who made the photographs of his late father Bert available to me, and to Wally Headington for his Home Guard memories and the photos of the ATA Home Guard unit and the White Waltham Battle of Britain parade.

# 1

# How it All Started

It all began for me in 1934 when I was three years old. I used to stand at the window at home - Meadowside, How Lane - watching lorries taking sand and gravel for the new buildings going up on the airfield site, close to the railway. The De Havilland School of Flying opened on the airfield in November 1935 - its hangars modelled on the De Havilland buildings at Hatfield.

By the outbreak of war in September 1939, the school had trained 500 pilots for the RAF. But the airfield's greatest days were yet to come. White Waltham became the headquarters of Air Transport Auxiliary - the civilian organisation which ferried over 300,000 aircraft from factories to airfields and RAF Maintenance Units in the UK.

Two factories were built in the village - Anti-Attrition Metal Company in Cannon Lane and ML Aviation, close to the parish church. The RAF established a ground station which at its peak housed over 2000 people and the Army set up a School of Aircraft Recognition to train searchlight and gunsite personnel to tell friend from foe.

A searchlight post was set up in one of my Uncle Walter's fields at Drift Road and the lights for a dummy airfield were placed in more of his fields on the other side of the road, together with posts to deter parachutists! At least one enemy plane found the dummy airfield and dropped a few bombs on it.

Four large houses in the village all played their part in the war and even the remains of the stable block of the demolished Heywood Manor became an engineering school for ATA and post-war housed WAAFs. An advertisement in the Maidenhead Advertiser of September 7, 1939, invited girls to apply to Mrs. Carlisle at The Smithy House, White Waltham, to become cooks or clerical assistants in the ATS, 3rd Berks

Company, Maidenhead Unit. Mrs. Carlisle was company commander.

Gas masks had been issued in 1938 at the time of the Munich crisis. Once the war started, they had to be carried everywhere you went. Ration books for food, and later for clothing, followed and everyone received an identity card. So many leaflets and forms arrived that Bill Green, landlord of the Royal Oak at Paley Street, said the war was nothing but "a pocketful of papers".

The few street lights in White Waltham and Woodlands Park were switched off and homes had to be blacked out with heavy curtains, or shutters made from tarred paper.

My father, George Tomlinson, bought a stirrup pump for £1 and my school friend, John French of Littlefield Green, and I made fire beaters to directions given in a Government leaflet.

The few cars in the village were used even less, once petrol was rationed - later in the war it was for "essential users" only. When my father's ration came down to five gallons for 13 weeks, he sold his car and bought a pony and trap.

Luxury goods disappeared from the shops, rationed items were for registered customers only. Other goods in short supply were kept under the counter for favoured customers only and the black market flourished.

National newspapers shrank in size because of paper rationing; radio news bulletins were increased to five a day and the BBC television service was shut down until the war ended.

The war dominated the news - and everything else. Security was top priority. Posters constantly reminded us that "Careless talk costs lives" or urged us to "Be like Dad - keep Mum".

The Knapp sisters, living near us at Paley Street, took security very seriously. When Lottie took a job at the Anti-Attrition factory, her sister Alice couldn't tell us what the job involved. We later discovered she was a cleaner.

White Waltham Home Guard Platoon was formed in May 1940 (see Chapter 3) and air raid wardens were enrolled under Mr. Ronald Inman, chief warden. Mr. Inman was parish clerk and ran a taxi service from

Netherclift - the house demolished to allow for the expansion of White Waltham School. There was an Auxiliary Fire Service unit at White Waltham Place, where Mr. Raymond Oppenheimer, once captain of White Waltham Cricket Club, lived. While Mr. Oppenheimer was serving in the RAF, the house was used by De Beers for diamond sorting. The following is based on an article which appeared in a De Beers company magazine:

> Most De Beers diamond sorting staff remained in London until the blitz of 1940. Shottesbrooke Park was rented to accommodate staff and diamond sorting continued in Louis Oppenheimer's home at White Waltham Place. Diamond sales, or Sights, continued to take place in No 8 Charterhouse Street, London, until 1941, when the building was destroyed by German bombers. The sorted diamonds were brought up to London in the boot of a hired Daimler. In the summer, Louis Oppenheimer sometimes sent some strawberries from White Waltham, too.
>
> Security did not seem to be paramount in the country. From the outside, the large safe in the corner of the sorting room was clearly visible. There was never a security escort in the Daimler!

The land occupied by the airfield was originally part of Shottesbrooke Estate and was acquired by the De Havilland Aircraft Company from Miss Nancy Oswald Smith. Her home, Shottesbrooke Park, housed wounded Polish soldiers at one point during the war and Czechoslovakian refugees immediately after the war. Concert parties from Paley Street entertained both groups.

The RAF built a large underground air-raid shelter close to the house. Two ex-RAF members stationed at White Waltham have spoken of "walking across the park to sick quarters", which were situated in Old Garden Cottage, next to Shottesbrooke Church.

Elsewhere in the village, security was a serious matter and few people knew what was going on in the factories, or what the role of the RAF station was. The fascination of writing this book has been to find out what was happening on our own doorstep from 1939-45. What I can't answer is the question I was asked when giving a talk about my research - "Why were so many war-time activities concentrated in such a small village?"

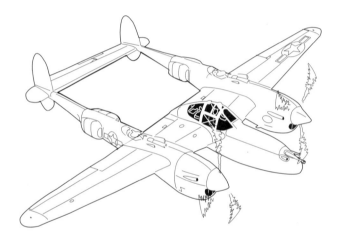

Lockheed Lightning

# 2

## "We're Building an Airfield"

One of the first families to be affected by the coming of the airfield were the Ewers family in Cherry Garden Lane.

Mr Edward Ewers had a house built in 1934. Soon after it was finished he saw men at work in the neighbouring field, pegging out land for buildings. He asked what they were doing. The answer: "We're building an airfield."

Mr Ewers had hoped to buy more land and start a nursery but increasing rheumatism and the onset of war meant these plans were never fulfilled. When the airfield was extended in 1943 it stretched across Cherry Garden Lane, so cutting the road in half. This meant that Mr Ewers' house, Oakfield, came within the perimeter of the airfield.

The Ewers family were issued with ATA passes to allow them through the airfield gate. Don Ewers' wife, living at Woodlands Park, was given a permit to use the Breadcroft Road gate once a week and walk behind the hangars to reach Oakfield.

When security officials came to check the house, Mrs Ewers had nine members of her family living at home. The officials asked: "Who else lives here?" She replied: "Where do you think we can put anyone else?" The officials did not come back.

Nissen huts and wooden huts were put up near the Ewers' home to house soldiers (later the RAF Regiment) and dog handlers responsible for guarding the aerodrome. The perimeter fence had barbed-wire entanglements behind it. The soldiers patrolled in personnel carriers at first but this was discontinued by 1943-44.

A German bomber machine-gunned the hangars one Sunday afternoon and Mrs Ewers was surprised that the soldiers in the gunpit at the bottom of her garden did not open fire. When she questioned them afterwards, the soldiers said their guns were trained on the plane but they were not allowed to fire without permission. Mrs Ewers said: "What, with all the cups of tea I have brought you, you couldn't even defend us".

Ken Ewers, photographed in 1948. The motor cycle, an Ariel Square Four, belonged to the author's brother John. Ken worked with John at ATA and later at Personal Plane Services, run by the late Doug Bianchi, servicing West London Aero Club aircraft. Afterwards Ken worked for ML Aviation.

The airfield opened as the De Havilland School of Flying in November 1935 with 21 silver and red Tiger Moth trainers and subsequently became the RAF's No 13 Elementary Flying Training School. It first carried out initial training for RAF pupil pilots and elementary and advanced training for reserve officers and NCOs. From April 1937 the school trained pilots for the RAF Volunteer Reserve. By 1939, it had 25 De Havilland Tiger Moths, now painted RAF yellow, plus other types, and 24 instructors - six of them part-time.

The coming of Air Transport Auxiliary to the airfield in February 1940 put pressure on the hangar space, and the white line which divided the hangar moved mysteriously to give ATA more and more space. The RAF flying school moved away to Peterborough in December 1940.

White Waltham was the headquarters of ATA. By the end of the war, pilots from the 16 ferry pools of this civilian organisation had ferried over 300,000 aircraft from factories to military airfields or RAF Maintenance Units.

Among the famous pilots based at White Waltham, which was No 1 Ferry Pool, were Amy Johnson, famed for her pre-war long-distance flights, and Jim Mollison, her former husband. Sadly, Amy Johnson drowned in the Thames Estuary while ferrying an Airspeed Oxford from Prestwick in Scotland to Kidlington, Oxfordshire, in bad weather.

Four engineers from British Airways came to White Waltham to form the nucleus of ATA's engineering section which was responsible for maintaining the taxi aircraft used to transport pilots to and from the factory airfields or their destinations. The most famous of these was the Avro Anson.

Many ground staff were recruited locally, including five members of the Ewers family - Joe, Jack, Don, Charlie and Ken, the youngest member of the family, who started in 1944. Charlie, who pre-war had delivered bread from White Waltham Bakery and Post Office, drove the ambulance to the relief airfield at Culham, near Henley-on-Thames, whenever flying was taking place there. He later moved, at De Havilland's request, to Witney.

A war-time shot of ATA ground staff at White Waltham, in front of a Vickers Warwick. Back row, seventh from left, Wally Headington; on his right, Jack Ewers; middle row, eighth from right, Fred Payne; front row, extreme right (hands on lap) Eric Jones; fifth from left, Dick Marshall.

My own brother John joined as a trainee engine fitter in July 1940 and worked for ATA until the rundown began in September 1945. The work was categorised as a "reserved occupation" - meaning that those in it were not allowed to join the armed forces. Among the 58 types he worked on, most of them during his time with ATA, was a variant of the Hawker Hart used by Prince Bernhard of the Netherlands until Dutch people in America presented him with a Beechcraft biplane.

Prince Bernhard had the honorary rank of Air Commodore in the RAF and was liaison officer for Dutch forces serving with the British. The Beechcraft was destroyed on the ground on an airfield near Brussels in a German air raid on January 1, 1945.

My brother has many memories of ATA, including the following:

- Being a member of the crash crew formed from hangar staff (before ATA had its own fire brigade and ambulance crews) and going to help the pilot of an Avro Commodore biplane which had crashed on the airfield in a gale. Don Ewers broke the fuselage to get the pilot out but the wing had damaged the fuel tank, located behind the pilot, and the petrol was running over his body and into his mouth; sadly, he died.

- Seeing a Flying Fortress crash on the airfield. The American crew had no idea where they were. The Americans sent a large mobile workshop, completely equipped, and within a week the badly damaged aircraft was repaired and flown out.

- Working on a Hawker Typhoon from Hawker's factory at Langley which had force landed with engine problems while on a test flight. Equipment was brought from Langley to lift out the 2200 horse power Napier Sabre engine.

The Langley factory, bought by Hawkers in 1936, opened in 1938. It made 7105 Hurricane fighters - almost half the total produced; 1349 Tempests, including four prototypes, and 15 production Typhoons.

ATA was responsible for ferrying all military aircraft from factories from April 1940. The object was to clear them as quickly as possible from the factories to reduce the risk of their being destroyed on the ground during air raids and to get them to operational airfields where they were urgently needed.

ATA pilots flew to many parts of Britain. The Langley factory and Miles Aircraft at Woodley were the nearest manufacturing plants to White Waltham. Nearly 1300 Magister training aircraft were made at Woodley from 1937-41 and many Spitfires were overhauled there. As ATA pilots were not allowed to fly after dark (they had no radio communication with the ground) any planes landed at dusk would be dispersed to the edges of the airfield.

The history of ATA has been well recorded - see booklist at end.

The Avro Anson, workhorse of ATA. Picture taken at Norwich Airport in 1970. (Photo ECN Library)

The pilots were mainly civilians but included up to 200 RAF pilots at any one time who, for one reason or another, were not on operational duties. The women flew all types of aircraft except flying boats; 11 were qualified to fly four-engined types including Lettice Curtis, author of The Forgotten Pilots, and Joan Hughes who later became an instructor with the West London Aero Club at White Waltham.

So long after the war, it is difficult to appreciate the size and scale of ATA's operations and the incredible job they did in keeping the RAF supplied with frontline aircraft.

Four-engined bombers were being produced at the rate of 400 a month by May 1943 and the Castle Bromwich factory near Birmingham, at its peak produced 320 Spitfires a month. The most aircraft moved on one day by ATA pilots was 570 - on February 21, 1945.

The people referred to affectionately as "Ancient and Tattered Aviators" deserve their place in history and helped to earn it for White Waltham.

Footnote. Lettice Curtis refers in her book to the many Air Training Corps cadets who had flights from White Waltham through ATA. She records that in 1942 an ATC Gliding School was set up by Eric and Rolf Pasold on the relief landing ground at Windsor Road, Bray. Rolf Pasold later joined ATA as a ferry pilot and Flight Lieutenant J.A. West became Commanding Officer of what was then No 3 Elementary Gliding School ATC. Gliding instruction for ATC cadets continued at White Waltham post-war.

A total of 1152 male pilots and 166 female pilots flew with ATA. The men, some in their 50s, were either over-age or unfit for operational duties.

# 3

## *The Home Guard on Patrol*

The Local Defence Volunteers (LDV) were formed as a result of a broadcast by Anthony Eden, Secretary of State for War, on May 14, 1940.

Age limits were 17-65, although some men under and over those ages enlisted. In the first 24 hours, 250,000 volunteered for the new force at local police stations.

By the end of June, there were 1½ million volunteers. The men had no weapons and no uniforms to start with - only an armband with the letters LDV on it. 250,000 of these armbands had been printed before the end of May.

The name LDV was changed to Home Guard following a broadcast on July 14, 1940, by the Prime Minister, Winston Churchill.

The White Waltham Platoon was formed at a meeting in Holly Cottage - the parish meeting room next door to the village post office - with Captain W. H. Bulteel in command. Fifty-three men enrolled.

There were enough volunteers to form seven patrols or sections - one to be on duty each night of the week from 8 p.m. to 6 a.m. Six corporals were appointed to take charge of the Sunday to Friday night patrols. Saturday was more difficult. To solve the problem, my father, George Tomlinson, agreed to take charge "if no-one else would."

He was a reluctant "soldier" but, like everyone else at the time, very worried about the threat of an invasion by Hitler's forces from just across the English Channel. And so he "did his bit".

My brother Brian, 17, volunteered and was in the Thursday night patrol until he joined the Royal Corps of Signals to train as a dispatch rider in November 1940, serving seven years as a regular soldier.

War-time pictures of the author's brothers - Brian (in uniform), a dispatch rider in the Royal Signals and John with his Norton motor cycle used in the Home Guard. Brian died in 1989.

My brother John joined in 1941 when he became 16. He had a motor cycle (a 1931 Norton 500 c.c. Model 18) and was the platoon dispatch rider with the rank of Lance-Corporal and received, I believe, an allowance of 1¼d (one and a quarter old pence) a mile for official duties. More valuable than the money were the few petrol coupons he received which enabled him to keep his motor cycle on the road. Petrol was rationed and no coupons were available for purely private motoring.

Unofficially, John used his motor cycle to go into Maidenhead to have his hair cut and, of course, wore his uniform on these occasions. As far as I know, he was never challenged when on this "duty".

The White Waltham platoon's first home was an Army hut built early in the war in Shottesbrooke Hill - a field belonging to my Uncle Walter who farmed How Lane Farm. The hut had housed the crew of a single searchlight set up on a concrete pad in the field.

While they were there, the soldiers were invited to nearby Buck Farm by the farmer, Mr Marshallsay, to have a bath as there was no bath at the hut. Later in the war, a much larger searchlight post was set up in the same field and the Home Guard moved to the other end of the village.

The first hut was half-a-mile from my home. Although rifles were not plentiful, the Home Guard at this stage, had two rifles and six shotguns. These were stored in the umbrella-stand just inside our front hall and were collected each evening by the patrol going on duty and returned next morning. My mother, Hilda Tomlinson, who had issued pens to schoolchildren when a teacher at White Waltham School, was no doubt surprised to find herself issuing shotguns to soldiers.

George Golding, who lived in Green Lane, came to the house each morning to clean the shotguns. If the guns had been fired, it was likely to have been "target practice" on a rabbit.

The patrol controlled the How Lane-Drift Road crossroads and the men on duty challenged anyone they thought suspicious. Hearing a pony and cart one night, my father's patrol, who had a shrewd idea who it was, called out "Halt." The reply, from a local gypsy, was: "It's only old Lee".

On another night my father challenged a couple in a parked car and asked to see their identity cards. The man produced his driving licence which read "His Grace the Duke of ----------."

When the searchlight post was re-established, the Home Guard moved to a wooden bungalow, formerly used as a chicken house, at Bowden's Farm in Butchers Lane, then to an old cottage in Cherry Garden Lane, next to North Lodge, also in Cherry Garden Lane, and finally to a Nissen hut not far from the main gate of the airfield and close to the western end of the hangar.

Their task was now to guard the railway bridge in Butchers Lane and to patrol the western side of the airfield. The bridge in Cherry Garden Lane was probably guarded by the airfield Home Guard platoon.

My brother John recalls: "We had no beds in the cottage and slept on the floor. It was cramped, to say the least, and we all had to turn over together when someone needed to change sides".

"Bob Mason, who was very much overweight and worked for Mr Hall, the village postmaster and baker, enjoyed the fun."

Both the cottage and North Lodge were demolished later in the war as the airfield was extended westwards to provide a longer runway for larger aircraft and more dispersal space, i.e. parking space for aircraft temporarily housed at White Waltham.

The extra space was necessary as the airfield sometimes received deliveries of Hurricanes late in the day from the Hawker factory at Langley, near Slough, which could not be delivered to airfields elsewhere until next day as ATA pilots were not allowed to fly in the dark. Other aircraft which could not reach their ultimate destination in daylight also stayed overnight.

As with other Home Guard platoons, White Waltham had its lighter moments. Christmas celebrations got out of hand one year. Sergeant Harry Smith went outside and fired his rifle at the moon. The village policeman, P.C. Jack Culver, cycled over to investigate. He was invited inside the Home Guard post, liberally entertained and lost all his money playing cards.

One night, a train on the main railway line was seen to be on fire. Two members of the platoon decided to investigate. Company Sergeant-Major Jack Garraway rode on the back of Sergeant Sid Smith's motor cycle combination. As they set off round the concrete perimeter track, they did not know that the track was unfinished. They came to an abrupt stop in wet concrete.

Another incident recalled by my brother John happened later in the war. By this time, the immediate threat of invasion had passed and older Home Guard members, including my father, were allowed to retire. Captain Fenwick now commanded the platoon. His day job was with a firm of wine merchants in London. He asked members of the platoon to report to Shottesbrooke Park one evening.

Their task was to pack bottles of wine which were racked into transport cases. They did it successfully and received a liquid reward afterwards. Jack Garraway was once asked by a Home Guard officer, Lt. Col. A.E. Marnham, of Holyport, "What would you do Garraway, if you saw a German armoured column advancing towards you?" Jack replied: "I'd get in my old lorry and drive as fast as possible in the opposite direction". The officer's final remarks are not recorded.

John remembers taking part in an attack on the Guards barracks at Windsor. "En route, we crossed a pig farm. Ken Golding trod in the manure up to his knees. I think the Guards smelled us coming."

John Hunt, a school friend of my brother's whose father was a chauffeur at White Waltham Place, also joined the Home Guard under age. John Hunt told me: "I went to see Capt. Bulteel. He said 'How old are you? I said 'I am 16.' Then he repeated the question and I again said 16. Capt. Bulteel then said 'I will ask you once more', so I said 17." John, who now lives in Harrogate, still has his Home Guard record card; he joined in July 1941. "We used to attack The Beehive on Sunday morning and captured it at about opening time."

Company Sergeant-Major Herbert Waite of the airfield Home Guard platoon. He once worked for De Havillands on the airfield and later in the armoury at RAF White Waltham. He and Lieutenant Ashplant (see Footnote on page 16) were also in a photograph of the Home Guard Women's Section published in *The Cut*, Spring 1979 issue. More about the Home Guard on pages 98-101.

The platoon's first sergeant major was Bob Leader, a former regular soldier, who lived at Cox Green. In their reminiscences published in *The Cut*, a magazine which circulated in White Waltham in the 1970s and early 80s, the late Bill Blay and Arthur Bushnell recalled that Bob was not impressed with the platoon's smartness.

Once he caught Gerald Strickland smoking on the march, halted the platoon, gave them a lecture, told them not to smoke and said he had never seen such a rag-tag lot in his life.

Capt. Louis Baylis, then editor of the Maidenhead Advertiser, also called White Waltham a rag-tag lot and was not impressed when only two members of the platoon - Tom Blay and Harry Smith - passed a map-reading test held in Maidenhead Drill Hall. "Come on, smarten up. Don't you know there's a war on?" he told them.

Sgt Britten, a Guards sergeant from Windsor, took the platoon on Sunday morning exercises, including an assault course at Downfield sandpits. He used live ammunition and practice grenades. When a grenade on the ground failed to explode, he detonated it with the butt of Tom Blay's rifle. It destroyed the butt, but prevented anyone stepping on the grenade. He took the rifle to Windsor and next week it had a new butt.

White Waltham Home Guard Platoon. Back row, left to right: Ted Smith, Dudley Clark, Bob Alexander, Arthur Bushnell, Gerald Strickland, Charlie Woodham, Wilf Moss, John Tomlinson. Middle row, left to right: Bill Blay (standing); Alfred (Benny) Young, Bill Clark, Reg Lawrence, Arthur Kent, Ernie Denton, Dick Ranscombe (standing). Front row, left to right: Bob Mason, Harry Smith, Jack Garraway, Captain Fenwick, Sid Smith, Percy Samways, Ken Golding.

Following the early days with the shotguns and two World War I Lee Enfield rifles, six Ross rifles were provided, also 1914 vintage, and later American Springfield rifles.

The Home Guard was stood down on December 31, 1944, but was not finally disbanded until a year later.

*(The source for national information given in this chapter is The Real Dad's Army by Norman Longmate, published by Arrow Books. My research has failed to find any details of the airfield Home Guard except that Lieutenant Ashplant and Sergeant-Major Herbert Waite served with the platoon).*

# 4

## School Days and the Flying Blackboard

I had been at White Waltham School for less than three years when the war started on September 3, 1939. Taking our gas masks to school every day became routine. Roy Smith recalls a gas mask inspection in class by the headmaster, Mr L. G. Bradfield.

"Our gas masks were in round tin containers. One girl had stood hers on the hot water pipe which ran round the classroom. When she opened it up, the rubber of the mask was stuck to the tin".

Two air raid shelters were built to protect us from air raids - one where the old bicycle shed had stood (it later became a coke store) and the other in the playground. Bill Blay, who died earlier this year, helped build them.

Before the shelters were built we practised diving under our desks for protection when the air raid siren sounded, which was not very often in daytime. When we went to the shelters, we sat on oval-shaped coconut mats. Tony Greening recalls playing his mouth organ in the shelter - something he also did on the first night of the London blitz, August 24, 1940, at his father's house near King's Cross. It was Tony's 12th birthday.

If there were no bombs falling on us, there could sometimes be dangers in class. Roy Smith recalls Mrs Bradfield reprimanding a boy at the back of the class who was not paying attention. She hit the blackboard so hard while doing so, that it fell off its easel on to Roy's desk. "I jumped up and put it back again. Mrs Bradfield said 'Thank you, Smith,' then resumed telling off the other boy in a very loud voice".

The arrival of evacuees from Holy Trinity School Paddington affected the school day. There were too many children all to be in school at the same time. So, for a while, local children went to school for mornings only one week, and afternoons only the next. The evacuees attended on the other half-days. The parish room at Holly Cottage served as an extra classroom.

One of Holy Trinity's teachers, Mrs Parsons, stayed in the area after the war when most evacuees had returned to London.

The Government, keen that children should be properly nourished despite food shortages, provided us with a third of a pint of milk free each day.

Quentin Todd, who had left school at Easter 1939 and was working for Mr A. J. Bucknell at Bury Court Farm, helped bottle the milk with Miss Olive Halfacre, who lived at Touchen End and worked on the farm. They delivered the milk to the school. One very cold winter, the milk froze in the bottles and raised the cardboard tops. "It was like an iced lolly", Roy Smith says. (We could still use the tap in the playground when we wanted a drink of water, providing it was not frozen).

Roy also had another job that winter. Because the water pipes were frozen, he and another boy had to take buckets of water to the toilets at the end of each playtime (break) to flush them. The flush toilets had only been installed in 1938.

White Waltham School, 1991.

School dinners were another innovation. Ours were cooked at Waltham St Lawrence School and brought in containers by van. Rice with dates was a favourite pudding of mine but semolina - ugh!

The annual Christmas party continued but to austerity standard. We made our own paper chains and took our own mugs to school. The school had no kitchen and no crockery of its own. We ate bread and jam (no butter or margarine) and buns, probably made without fat, from Mr Hall, the village postmaster and baker. All the children received a present of one shilling (five new pence) from Mr Raymond Oppenheimer of White Waltham Place. The shilling (12 old pence) represented 12 times most children's weekly pocket money and would almost pay for the cheapest seat at the Plaza cinema in Maidenhead's Queen Street. Games at the party included pinning the tail on the donkey.

The older boys went one afternoon a week to the school garden in Butchers Lane - just beyond the council houses. One afternoon I was walking along with a fork over my shoulder when an RAF lorry touched the fork, swinging the handle round into my face. It pushed back one of my lower teeth and it was never straightened by the school dentist. His base was the Old Drill Hall in Marlow Road, Maidenhead. He wore a thick tweed suit and heavy shoes; as he walked down the hall, you knew your fate was sealed.

The headmaster's car was off the road during the war as he received no petrol ration. Roy Smith was once asked to take his bicycle to Hammants garage at Woodlands Park for a puncture to be repaired. "It was a big old bike and I was supposed to walk with it but, or course, I rode with one leg through the crossbar. This didn't do the tyre much good and when Mr Bradfield went to collect it, he had to pay for a new tyre. I never got the job again".

With the wide variety of aircraft that flew in and out of the airfield, aeroplane spotting (identifying the different types) was popular with boys. We also played aeroplanes in the playground and drew aeroplanes in class. Ken Ewers, who in retirement has taken up painting, was always the best artist.

The most romantic aircraft of the time was the Spitfire. One ex-pupil, Bert Goodchild, learned to fly after the war and eventually flew a Spitfire.

Bert and his twin brother Ron were members of a family of six, all of whom attended White Waltham School. With their brothers Bill, Francis, Maurice and sister Joyce, they were at the reunion of former pupils held at White Waltham School on October 24, 1997.

Ron was a messenger on the airfield and put in many hours as a flight assistant on ATA aircraft, operating flaps and undercarriage. On call-up in 1944 he was unable to get into the RAF and joined the Royal Wiltshire Regiment.

Bert's call-up was deferred until 1946 because he worked at ML Aviation. He was conscripted for the mines as a Bevin Boy but managed to get into the RAF before going down the mines. (Bevin Boys, 82,000 in all, were selected by ballot and directed to work in the mines as an alternative to serving in the Forces). Bert served his 18 months as a flight mechanic (airframes).

On leaving the RAF in May 1948, he worked for Fairey Aviation at White Waltham and became a spare-time airman with 601 Squadron of the Royal Auxiliary Air Force at Hendon. He was called back for three months full-time service during the Korean crisis in the early 1950s.

He gained his pilot's licence with the West London Aero Club in 1949. His instructor was Joan Hughes, the former ATA instructor, who was one of the first women in ATA to fly four-engined bombers.

Bert Goodchild in the cockpit of a Spitfire Mark IX, May 1978.

Bert finally achieved his ambition to fly a Spitfire in 1970 at the age of 43 - his childhood dream come true. In 1998 he was still working part-time for British Airways Flying Club at Wycombe Air Park, Booker Airfield, occasionally flying a De Havilland Chipmunk and Cessnas.

TONY GREENING, who was at White Waltham School from 1938-40 was living with an aunt at Woodlands Park when the war started. He clearly remembers the air raid on the aerodrome by a Dornier bomber in July 1940. He was walking home from school along the Waltham Road to Woodlands Park with two younger boys, Maurice Goodchild and Leslie Rogers.

"We knew what the plane was, because we were all aircraft enthusiasts. It dropped a stick of bombs on the airfield. As it turned round, I dragged Maurice, who was crying, and Les into Mr Wingrove's cornfield opposite the airfield.

The Dornier dropped more bombs on the airfield before flying south. We heard later it had been shot down.

"I was at the bus stop opposite Hammants Garage when two Bristol Blenheims collided overhead. One came up under the other and took the tail off. One came down behind a bungalow closer to Cox Green; the pilot was on his first solo flight.

The other came down in a field just off Woodlands Park Avenue. I dashed through the gardens to get to it and saw Harry Hunter (father of George Hunter, a White Waltham School pupil) who asked for my penknife to free an occupant from his harness, but unfortunately it was too late. One trainee pilot and an instructor died. Then the rescue people came and took over".

Tony recalls traffic being held up on the Waltham Road at Woodlands Park while aircraft were taxied from the airfield across the road into the grounds of Heywood Manor where ATA had a hangar which later became Woodlands Park's first village hall.

Tony helped put out incendiary bombs dropped on the airfield and surrounding area late one night by a German aircraft.

"No actual damage was done but the hangars were lit up by dozens of small fires from the bombs buried in the soft ground of the airfield.

The Goodchild brothers, Ron and Bert, and I went out on to the airfield and extinguished as many as we could by kicking earth on top of them.

A truck drove out to us and one of the occupants thanked us but warned us to be careful. He was Gerard d'Erlanger, head of ATA, who post-war became head of British European Airways.

Bert Goodchild airborne in a De Havilland Rapide G - AKIF.

Next morning, I found an unexploded incendiary lying on its side, in perfect condition, in soft earth in our back garden. I had ideas of disarming it by unscrewing the detonator and took it indoors and was kicked out smartly. So I took it round to the Goodchilds and was kicked out even more smartly, and told to take it to the main gates of the airfield in Cherry Garden Lane, and let them deal with it.

So I took it, hanging from the handlebars of my bike, and gave it to a soldier guarding the gate. He went quite pale, and that was the last I saw of it".

On leaving school in 1942, Tony was offered two jobs - one with a firm of shipping brokers evacuated from Leadenhall Street, London, to the Hotel de Paris in Bray, at £1.25 a fortnight; the other with Anti-Attrition

Metal Company at Woodlands Park (see chapter 5) at £1.37½p a week. He went to Anti-Attrition, became a millwright's improver and was exempt from call-up until 1946.

He had been a member of the Air Training Corps but went into REME, the Royal Electrical and Mechanical Engineers, serving as a welder in Germany with BAOR (British Army of the Rhine). On demob in 1949, he worked as a sprayer for two years with West London Aero Club before returning to his old trade as a coded welder and steel fabricator.

His later father-in-law, Alf Friend, was a London employee of Anti-Attrition. He and his wife and two daughters moved to Maidenhead after a V2 rocket destroyed their home in Trafalgar Avenue, Peckham.

Daughter Mary, who Tony married in 1950, was a typist in the factory office before joining the Women's Land Army. She worked for Mr Walter Tomlinson (the author's uncle) at How Lane Farm, Paley Street, and also for the Ewart family at Waltham St Lawrence and ICI at Jealotts Hill.

At the age of 40, Tony took up motor cycle sidecar racing as a hobby and has 60 trophies as a record of his considerable success in the sport.

North-American Mustang

# 5

## Jobs for the Girls at Anti-Attrition

The Anti-Attrition Metal Company was formed in 1936. It had two factories - one at Peckham in South-east London that was bombed and badly damaged during the war and the other at Cannon Lane, Woodlands Park. The Woodlands Park factory made bushes\* of all sizes for aircraft engines and large castings for railway locomotives and employed over 100 staff.

A third of the women employees were local girls. Some came from London and lived in a house on the corner of All Saints Avenue and St Mark's Road, called Amco House. It had been bought by the company. There was another hostel in Newlands Drive. Most of the London girls went home at weekends.

By 1960 the company had become part of Beyer Peacock. The company was moved to Manchester in 1961-62 and closed down in 1966. The premises at Woodlands Park were occupied for a time by Black and Decker but were eventually demolished. Today, the site is known as Foundation Park and houses a number of separate businesses.

Chairman and managing director of Anti-Attrition was the late Steve Loosen. His son Stanley, who has now also died, was junior director in charge of the general running and administration of the factory. Stanley's secretary from 1946-49 was Mavis Winfield.

She joined in 1942, working first in the machine office and then in the upstairs offices. Her first job was with the OB department, concerned with parts for the overhead trolleys. Later she typed AID (Aircraft Inspection Directorate) forms. AID inspectors visited the factory from time to time. Her husband Leslie joined the factory after leaving the

---

\* bush: a box or bearing in which a shaft revolves.

Forces and became foreman of the new production of centrifugal castings. The Loosens are remembered by having a road at Cox Green - Loosen Drive - named after them.

Loosen Drive, the road at Cox Green named after the Loosen family.

ANN AIKEN (nee Wells), who had worked in domestic service at Waltham St Lawrence after leaving White Waltham School, heard that the new factory at Woodlands Park was doing war work. With her sister, the late Mrs Edith Walters, she applied and was taken on as a machine operator in the machine shop at 31s. 8d. a week - three times her wage as a housemaid. This was February 1942. She stayed until she married in August 1946.

Ann writes: "My sister was soon transferred to the inspection room but I stayed in the machine shop. There weren't many machines or girls there then but each week saw more and more arriving.

We started work at 8 a.m. and my clocking-in number was 80. Each employee was given an enamel badge to wear, indicating that they were on National Service at the Anti-Attrition.

Factory work classified of national importance was an option for girls who would otherwise have been called up for the Forces or joined the Women's Land Army or moved into other essential work such as the hospital service.

We worked until 5.30 p.m. with ten-minute breaks morning and afternoon and an hour for lunch. I normally lunched in the canteen, but after finding a caterpillar in the cabbage one day, I cycled home to lunch each day - 20 minutes each way.

The noise of the machines was unbearable at first and it took most girls some time to get used to it - often we'd go home with splitting headaches. As the machine shop was heated by several large coke furnaces, at times it was just like working in a thick pea-soup fog.

As the war went on and we became busier, we did overtime until 7.30 p.m., Saturday mornings until 12 noon and even some Sundays from 9 a.m. to 4 p.m. The top wage for girls over 21 was something over £2 a week.

I was one of a group of eight girls who went on night work for the first time. After a while it became two shifts a month on day work and a month on nights.

I worked on a number of different machines - some very old ones from the First World War. Some of the old machines were replaced with new Ward capstan lathes. It was hard work and very tiring, but I suppose we thought we were 'doing our bit' to help brothers, husbands or boyfriends who were serving in the Forces.

We only had a half-hour of BBC radio's Music While you Work broadcast over the Tannoy system morning and afternoon. The air-raid warnings were also sounded over the Tannoy but we were not allowed to leave our machines. Only once do I remember being told to go to the basement canteen, which served as our air-raid shelter.

During our morning break we could get a cup of tea and a bun in the canteen for a few pence. A cooked lunch cost ten old pence and a sweet two old pence.

At one stage, six girls were sent from Coventry to work at the Anti-Attrition. We heard they had been doing the same work as us but had been bombed out. After a few weeks we heard they were being paid double our wages. The foreman agreed this was true so a large number of girls said this was unfair.

The foreman wouldn't do anything about it so we asked to see Stanley

Loosen, the junior director who ran the factory. I was one of eight girls who waited outside his office for half-an-hour. He asked us in and explained that the Coventry girls had been earning the higher wage back home so he had to pay it. He agreed that we should get the same money and he said he would see what he could do. After two or three days, the Coventry girls went back - but we didn't get any more money!"

An early post-war group at the Anti-Attrition factory. Left to right: (Man in cap not known); Leslie Winfield, Stanley Loosen, junior director; Stanley Platt, town clerk of Maidenhead; Maidenhead Alderman Harold Neve; Alderman Walter Palmer, Mayor of Maidenhead; Steve Loosen, chairman and managing director.

Vi Frape (nee Young) also worked at Anti-Attrition as a capstan lathe operator and shares many of Ann Aiken's memories. When on night shift, she worked continuously through the night.

Vi started at the factory in 1940 and stayed for another 2½ years after she married in 1945. She and Ann, who have remained friends through the years, both married airmen stationed at RAF White Waltham.
Ann recalls some of the machines used in the factory - Herberts, several

sizes of Wards of which her favourite was the Ward 2A. The Drummond was large so that Ann, only 5ft 1in, could not see over the top of it. "When the war was over, we had an aeroplane engine, sliced in half, sent to us so that we could see where all the different bushes went that we had been making". The large Ward 10 machine made brass rings for the Royal Navy.

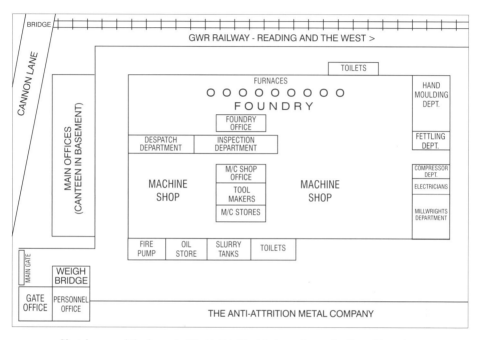

Sketch map of the layout of Anti-Attrition factory, drawn by Tony Greening.

Tony Greening (biographical details chapter 4) worked at the factory as a millwright's improver from September 1942 to September 1945. He has supplied the detailed plan on Anti-Attrition as he remembers it. Among his memories are the following:

"In 1944 I argued for, and was reluctantly given, a pay rise of one shilling (5p) per week. As we worked a 48-hour week, this worked out at one farthing per hour.

The machine operators at Anti-Attrition were girls, the machine tool setters men. They made bushes of all sizes for aircraft engines and large castings for railway locomotives.
One of the company directors was Alderman Round, Mayor of

Camberwell. His daughter married Stanley Loosen, whose father, Steven Loosen, was chairman and managing director".

Tony remembers a Workers' Playtime broadcast and the BBC Home Service (forerunner of Radio 4) being made from the factory with Bryan Michie or Bill Gates as compere. Top of the bill was George Robey, the "Prime Minister of Mirth".

Dances in the canteen were to Phil's Pioneers, a band from the Pioneer Corps, whose accordionist was Freddie Destephano.

Foundation Park - built on the site of the Anti-Attrition factory. During the war, lorries delivering to the factory sometimes went to Cannon Court Road, Maidenhead, by mistake and had to be redirected.

# 6

## ML Aviation's War-time Role

HUSH-HUSH is probably the best word to describe the work undertaken by R. Malcolm in the factory put up in 1940, not far from the parish church, and conveniently sited on the edge of the airfield. The company did not change its name to ML Aviation until 1946.

It had grown out of two pre-war companies: Wrightson Aircraft Sales, formed in 1934, and the R. Malcolm company, formed in 1936. It was Malcolm's, as the company was known in the village, which carried out aircraft product work.

Marcelle Lobelle, who had been chief designer for Fairey Aviation and had designed the Fairey Swordfish, joined Malcolm's early in the war. He supervised the drawing office in Slough which was working for the Ministry of Aircraft Production on development work.

In his publication Aviation History at White Waltham, A. J. Clark writes: "In order to operate the expanding design and experimental work more efficiently, the drawing office and experimental work were moved to White Waltham".

The building put up to house this work, which was itself a hangar and later had offices built inside, was second in size only to the hangars on White Waltham airfield.

Ronnie Malcolm, as he was known, left the company in 1943 and became a ferry pilot with ATA.

Work undertaken by Malcolm's during the war is listed by Mr Clark as follows:

    A wide range of jettisonable hoods for fighter aircraft.

Towing hooks and tow ropes with quick release gear for use with gliders and their aircraft which were extensively used for D-Day and subsequent airborne landings.

Personnel mine blast protection shoe.

Battle tank recovery/retrieval hook.

Pick-up equipment by which a man was snatched from the ground without the aircraft having to land.

The fitting of a rotor to a jeep to enable it to become airborne when towed by an aircraft.

In his book RAF Coastal Command 1936-1969 (Patrick Stephens), Chris Ashworth records that Hawker Hurricane Mark IIs were modified for meteorological work by Malcolm's in 1944. They went to 1402 Flight at Aldergrove, Northern Ireland.

Marcel Lobelle, chief designer, inspecting an aircraft handler for use on an aircraft carrier or on land. He was formerly chief designer for Fairey Aviation and was the "L" of ML.

After the war, ML worked on the development of ejector seats and had a Meteor aircraft behind its buildings as a test rig for the seats. Many other projects followed and the company rapidly expanded from the

1950s. With its talented team of design engineers, it remained in the forefront of companies producing aviation products for the defence industry.

ML Aviation left White Waltham in 1989-90 after taking over Wallop Industries at Andover. ML was merged into Flight Refuelling Ltd, as part of the Military Systems Division in 1997 and Flight Refuelling Ltd is a company within Cobham PLC, both based at Wimborne in Dorset.

Photographed behind the main ML Aviation building, a North American Mustang fighter fitted with Malcolm bubble cockpit hood. This gave much better visibility for the pilot when in operation. Most Allied fighters were fitted with a bubble hood made by Malcolms.

ML (as was) continues to have a presence at White Waltham in the form of a small but highly trained team of engineers who test products designed for deployment on such aircraft as Tornado and Eurofighter - for the next millennium.

Approval was given in 1996 for the White Waltham ML site to be redeveloped and shortly afterwards, in June 1996, the buildings were badly damaged in an arson attack.

The largest of the new units on the site was, on completion, occupied by Hewland Engineering, which manufactures gearboxes and transmission components for racing cars. ML (Engineering) remained in Slough until 1997 when it moved to Andover.

Aerial view of the ML site in the early 1980s. The white buildings on the left were formerly part of the RAF station's NAAFI canteen.

*Footnote. A display of products made by ML, with notes on the company's history, is located at the Museum of Berkshire Aviation, Mohawk Way, Woodley, near Reading. It has been prepared by Dick Gordon, a design engineer with ML from 1959-98. In retirement, he sees this as a way of securing permanent recognition for the company which was his life for so many years.*

# 7

## One of Ours or One of Theirs?

The Royal Artillery ran a School of Aircraft Recognition, sited on the Waltham Road, opposite the airfield. Its purpose was to train ATS girls and soldiers serving on searchlight and anti-aircraft gun sites in aircraft recognition.

One of the instructors at the school was Sergeant William Trotman. He kept close links with ATA on the airfield and arranged flights in an Avro Anson for people who topped his courses. He once lectured to White Waltham Home Guard platoon on aircraft recognition. Ken Ewers (see Chapter 2) recalls hearing him broadcast on the radio, making use of his expert knowledge of aircraft recognition. This could have been in the regular Ack-Ack Beer-Beer programme, which was aimed at gunsite and barrage balloon personnel. The Radio Times shows that there were aircraft recognition quizzes on the programme.

Charlie Hedges, then a pupil at White Waltham School, recalls taking library books supplied by Holyport Branch of the (Royal) British Legion to the School of Aircraft Recognition. Post-war, the wooden huts which were the lecture rooms and the Nissen huts which formed the living quarters were occupied by squatters - mostly returning Servicemen and their families who could not find a house or flat. The huts were later taken over by Cookham Rural District Council, the local housing authority, and huts were allocated to families on their waiting list.

Mrs Vi Frape of Woodlands Park lived in one of the huts for 4½ years until she was allocated a council house; one of her daughters was born there. The rent, in 1947, was 25p a week (five shillings). "Most of the huts were tin, but mine was a big wooden one at the entrance to the main road, with divided rooms and a kitchen range. We had to fetch water from a tap. The huts had electric lighting and a bucket toilet. They were the good old days and we enjoyed it", she recalls. As council houses became available to tenants, the site was gradually cleared.

Jean Harman (nee Green) attended the School of Aircraft Recognition twice - in February 1943 and for a Spotters Refresher Course from May 8-13, 1944. She remembers Sgt Trotman as short, dark and quite a character. It was said that the School was his idea and that he was someone of note at the Royal Aircraft Establishment, Farnborough, though this may be apocryphal.

```
Tel. No:    Seven Kings 5588

Subject:    Course.

To: -       W/1180755 Pte. Green. J.I.


            You will attend Course Serial R8/8 - Spotters Refresher Course,
at 1 AA Gp (M) Trg Est, Recognition Wing, White Waltham, Maidenhead, for
the period 8 - 13 May 44.

            You will take kit as detailed together with notebooks and
pencils.    You will hand in Health Certificate and return railway warrant
on arrival.
            Train Timings. - Romford  dep 13.48    Liverpool St  arr 14.14
                              Paddington dep 13.12  Maidenhead    arr 13.58


Whalebone Lane North,
ROMFORD, Essex.                      Margaret W Dickey
8 May 44                                  Subs/Major R.A.,
A.G.P.                               Commanding 532 (M)H.A.A. Battery R.A.,
```

Jean Harman's instructions to attend the Spotters Refresher Course at White Waltham.

"Several of us visited White Waltham airfield with Sgt Trotman. He showed us around a Hawker Hind, Miles Magister, Hawker Hurricane, Handley-Page Hampden, Lockheed Hudson and Vickers Wellington. We were able to go inside the larger aircraft and we sat in an Avro Anson while he explained the controls and how to fly it. We caught his enthusiasm and thoroughly enjoyed the day. I wasn't one of the lucky ones who had a flight in an Anson," Jean has written.

Jean also has a faint memory of the Barn Canteen as being converted stables. "I seem to remember the tables were in the old stalls. The meal we had was good for those times - some sort of mixed grill, I think."

Jean still has her original posting notice to the 1944 course she attended, which is identified as "Course Serial R8/8 - Spotters Refresher Course at 1 AA Gp (M) Trg Est, Recognition Wing, White Waltham, Maidenhead." She was instructed to take her kit as detailed together with notebooks and pencils and hand in her health certificate and return railway warrant on arrival.

She had to wait until 1950 for her flight over White Waltham. This was at an air display when she went for a joy ride in a De Havilland 86. Jean also has a cutting showing a photograph of a class in session at the School which includes Joan (surname unknown) - a spotter in her battery, No. 532. She also recalls a Sgt Davies who was on the permanent staff at the School.

Mrs A. P. Mason joined the ATS as Volunteer Elliott, A. P., W/26692, rank Private. Most of her service was spent on gunsites but for a year she was on the permanent staff at White Waltham. She recalls Jim Mollison as one of the ATA ferry pilots operating from the airfield, just across the road from the School. "They also had Spitfire pilots who had face and hands burnt. They were resting from operational duties before they went for a skin graft or plastic surgery with the famous surgeon, Sir Archibald McIndoe, There were some very brave men there", she writes.

Mrs Mason was at White Waltham when the first Americans came to Maidenhead. The ATS gave a party for children from the villages whose dads were in the Forces. "I made sweets and cakes for the party. When the Americans, who we met off duty, were told about the party, some of their officers, sergeants and men brought candy, oranges, all sorts of fruit and ice cream with them, and cartoon films. Some of the children had never seen ice cream or had a banana as ice cream was not made in Britain during the war and bananas were non-existent. The Americans even helped put the little ones on their potties. It was great fun".

Mrs Mason remembers that Queen Wilhelmina of the Netherlands lived at Stubbings House, Pinkneys Green, and used to go shopping in Maidenhead. She also saw Prince Bernhard in his white sports car with a Dalmatian in the front passenger seat.

She says that the American Flying Fortress which made an emergency landing on the airfield still had ammunition in its guns. The Americans gave bullets to some of the students at the School who were going back to their batteries. When this was discovered, they had to be taken off the train, their kitbags searched and the bullets removed.

Helen Moore, who attended a course at the School in 1942, writes as follows:

"In the summer of 1942, I was a member of A Troop, 495 Battery, 93rd Searchlight Regiment, Royal Artillery, stationed on a small site in Welders Lane, Chalfont St Peter, Buckinghamshire. We were the first detachment to take over a site from the male Gunners, having been specially trained as an experiment at Kinmel Park, Rhyl.

I had a book on aircraft recognition and whilst we were talking to the Troop Commander (Mrs Scott) in the field outside, a twin-bodied (or twin-boom) aircraft flew over and I dived for cover - I thought it was a Focke-Wulf I had seen in the book. Mrs Scott was very impressed and arranged for me to go to White Waltham on an aircraft recognition course".

One of Helen's disappointments during the course was that, because of bad weather, the A T S girls were unable to go up in Tiger Moths to see the effect of searchlights on aircraft crews. The other bad memory is of peeling large tubs of potatoes - a job the girls did in rotation for the whole camp. On the searchlight site at Jordans where she had come from, they had their own kitchen orderly.

"We did not have any men on our site, nor did we have guns. We were in a fighter zone; we illuminated targets to be shot down by the RAF. We later went on to plot and spot V1 flying bombs. As we were in the Royal Artillery, we were known as 'Gunners' in the first instance, and we were very proud to wear the Sword of London on our arms - it pierced a Dornier aircraft.

Later on we all became 'Privates' in the ATS and the symbol on our sleeve became a red square with a bow and arrow in black. We were not pleased about this as we felt rather apart from the rest - no men to help us!

We did our own spotting and plotting which some sites relayed to RAF Uxbridge via Swakeleys House, Ickenham, Middlesex - our Battery H.Q."

Helen Moore's maiden name was Pilkington and she left the Army as Sgt Parker. She later remarried but is now a widow. She served on many sites including Moor Park, Rickmansworth, Windsor Great Park, Staines, Sudbury Hill, Farnham Common, Sidcup and Hayling Island.

Helen sent me a history of the 93rd Searchlight Regiment - the only Searchlight Regiment to be manned by women. Its official designation was 93rd (M) S/L Regt., R. A. The history, by Mrs P. E. Longland, formerly Subaltern P.E. Baxter, ATS, makes the point that as well as illuminating enemy aircraft, the searchlights could also provide a homing beacon for crippled friendly aircraft returning from operations over France and Germany. "A permanent hazard was the fact that enemy aircraft would fire along the aircraft beam to extinguish it," the history states.

Margaret Schulman served as Subaltern M.A. Browne in 450 (M) Heavy Anti-Aircraft Battery which was stationed at Loughton, Essex, and subsequently sent to the Romney Marshes to combat flying bombs. After D-Day, the battery went to Belgium as part of the defence of Brussels.

She attended the School of Aircraft Recognition, in spring or autumn 1943 and really enjoyed it. "I was especially pleased at the final test on the course to gain one of the highest marks. It was, of course, a mixed class. I remember being near to the ATA organisation and being very impressed by the fact that there were numerous women involved," she said. As it was a short course (one or two weeks was usual) there was not the temptation to go off site, so she did not visit the village.

PUTTING THE PIECES TOGETHER. Anti-Aircraft Command Group Recognition Schools employ many novel methods of aircraft recognition instruction. This model "breaks down" into its component parts and is used for explaining technical terms and details of aircraft construction.

This photograph, taken at White Waltham, appeared in a war-time magazine. The instructor is Captain Smith.

Mrs Joan Aldam also has happy memories of her time at the School and, in her words, the lovely countryside surrounding the camp. She went on a spotters' refresher course which started on September 1, 1943, and went back for a two weeks' instructor's course on November 22, 1943. There was the chance of a flight in an ATA Anson at the end of the course. Names were put in a box and the first six to be drawn went up. "When I went up, there was a second aircraft and my name was first out," Joan said. "It was a very hot day and I was very frightened by the noise of the plane. The last time I was there, I got 100% in the closing test. I was Private Joan Cowell (Service number 123155) and I was with 532 (M) AA Battery, Whalebone Lane North, Romford, Essex." Joan joined the ATS at the age of 18. She is second from left in the picture on page 39.

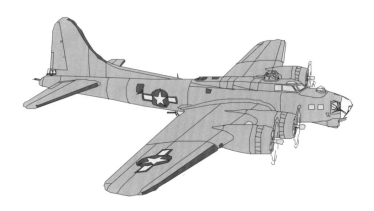

Flying Fortress

# 8

## Keeping the Planes Flying

Chapter 2 describes the work of Air Transport Auxiliary. To keep the taxi aircraft and military aircraft in transit flying, an efficient spare parts system was needed. This was centred on White Waltham airfield where an equipment section to provide the spares was operated by some 50 RAF and WAAF (Women's Auxiliary Air Force) Personnel.

A wide range of spares was held in stock for the many types of aircraft being ferried, plus the taxi aircraft. Their job was to deliver and collect the ferry pilots from their ferry pools to the factory airfields or service airfields.

The engineers at White Waltham drew their spares from this store and spares were sent to other parts of the UK as needed by rail, road or air. ATA drivers from White Waltham drove to mainline rail terminuses in London with parcels to catch overnight trains. The regular deliveries by ATA Ansons went direct to the airfields where they were needed, with a WAAF equipment assistant on board. This was known as the AOG (Aircraft on Ground) service.

Warrant Officer Ron Mutton, who served in the equipment section from 1943-45 and now lives in Cornwall, told me: "Sometimes a new aircraft being delivered to a squadron, because of some trouble, had to land somewhere other than its destination.

Then, the AOG procedure came into operation and an Anson was sent to collect and deliver the spares required. The equipment section operated during working hours. At night, there was an NCO (Non-commissioned Officer)* and one or more equipment assistants available for any urgent request during the night. The delivery Anson would fly off at first light next day.

* Sergeant, Corporal etc.

The telephone exchange was manned by WAAF personnel 24 hours a day, including weekends.

Speaking of his arrival at White Waltham, after five years in Karachi, in what is now Pakistan, Ron Mutton said: "It was quite an experience. This was my first experience of war-time Britain and having to deal with personnel of both sexes.

I did some visits to the scattered ferry pools in a Fairchild Argus. My pilot was usually a small youngish South American lady. She was very good. We had some sticky moments, but survived.

During the three years I was at White Waltham, we had no connection with RAF White Waltham. The equipment section came under H.Q. No. 41 Group at Andover and their officers came down at intervals to look around.

Because it was a unique set-up, we were left on our own under our commanding officer - at that time, Squadron Leader Pip (Philip) Morgan and later, Squadron Leader Turner.

There is no doubt we were greatly appreciated by the ATA, especially by the boss of the ATA engineers at White Waltham.

The RAF men in the equipment section were billeted in huts on the ATA site. Some married personnel were accommodated with their families in local houses or flats.

The WAAFs lived in The Hockett - a large country house four miles away at Cookham Dean and were brought to the airfield each day in an ATA bus driven by RAF personnel and returned at the end of their shift".

The bus also took them to Maidenhead for dances and other social outings. When The Hockett was closed, before ATA was disbanded, the remaining WAAFs were billeted at White Waltham. The Hockett later became the official residence of the Air Officer Commanding-in-Chief of Reserve Command, later renamed Home Command.

Four of the WAAFs who served in the equipment section have supplied their reminiscences. Doris Harris (nee Tee) re-established contact with three former colleagues by an advertisement in Airmail, magazine of the Royal Air Forces Association. Doris was an equipment assistant, working mainly in equipment accounts.

She recalls walking from The Hockett to a pub in the village, probably the Jolly Farmer, and also through the woods to Marlow for church parades. "We went to dances in Maidenhead with the Americans, the ATA bus taking us there and back".

Doris Harris (nee Tee) in the cabin of an Avro Anson. The parcel she is holding has an AOG (Aircraft on Ground) label on it.

Doris flew on AOG trips in an Anson - "one day out, stay a night in Kirkbride, then back next day. We carried urgently-needed spares, sometimes mail and quite often people. I flew with many ATA pilots.

I also attended New Year's Eve parties at Altmore - the country house in Cherry Garden Lane, not far from the airfield entrance. We spent some evenings in Maidenhead at the Canteen Club and also visited the

Bear Hotel, Riviera Hotel, Skindles and the Thames Hotel. We also went to dances at the Canadian Red Cross Hospital at Taplow.

Several of us who were Catholics went to Midnight Mass at St Joseph's in Maidenhead. It was a long walk back to The Hockett. In our free time, we often went to London and I went home to Guildford when possible as it was easy to hitch a lift. If I missed the train at Maidenhead and my connection at Reading, I would sleep on the station for the night.

The benches were very hard but at least in those days we were reasonably safe. We all looked after one another".

Pamela Fletcher, (then Meekcoms), now living in Canada, was at White Waltham from 1942-43 as an equipment assistant. Unlike some of the other WAAFs she did not regard her posting to White Waltham as the best in the world.

"I came straight from an equipment course. I was not cut out for office work which unfortunately was my lot! I hated the civilians correcting our efforts, so hence I was bored stiff". Pamela used the Barn Canteen, by White Waltham Church. She also recalls the 1943 New Year party given by ATA.

"The food was out of this world. I know to this WAAF it was heaven. Just things you never saw in war-time and certainly never saw again for the rest of the war, plus free drinks. I missed the bus back to The Hockett.

We had a sports event at The Hockett which I took part in and fell flat on my face in a race".

Beryl Smallwood (nee Waller) was, for most of her time, the only clerk (general duties) in the equipment section. Another clerk (general duties), who became a Corporal, worked in the section for a short time. She worked first for Flight Lieutenant (later Squadron Leader) Pip Morgan and then in the orderly room.

"After being stationed at HQ No. 41 Group, Andover, living at The Hockett was much nicer. After we complained of the food at the nearest RAF station, we then had our meals at The Hockett.

The cook there was named Waller and was a highly-trained civilian cook. All the American boys stationed near Maidenhead wanted to come for dinner on Sundays when we could invite guests".

Of Pip Morgan she says: He was a great person to work for. Pre-war, Beryl worked at Erlangers bank in the City of London - the family bank of which Commodore Gerard d'Erlanger, head of ATA, was a member. The bank was very good to employees joining up, making up their Service pay to civilian levels, she recalls.

"I know that the WAAF's at The Hockett were the envy of other WAAF personnel at nearby camps for living in a beautiful house. Rumours were rampant that we were chosen for our looks.

My husband went to join the RAF at Halton as an apprentice and was overseas for nine years before transferring to the Royal Canadian Air Force after we married in 1944. I was a war bride and went to Canada in March 1946. Never regretted it and never visited England again".

Corporal Iris Doney (nee Scott) arrived in Spring 1943 from Amport, just outside Andover. She was first taken to RAF White Waltham, but after much confusion and phone calls went to ATA and was billeted at The Hockett. She worked in the main equipment section office, keeping track of the ins and outs of equipment passing between the ferry pools in England and Scotland.

"I had never had a sitting-down job before in my life, but I really enjoyed it. The office was large, with windows on three sides and my desk in the middle", Iris said.

Corporal Iris Doney (nee Scott).

She remembers Bert Stubbs and a red-headed Scot called Jock as drivers of the ATA bus which took the WAAFs to and from The Hockett. There were three Gwens in the equipment section - Gwen Collier; Gwen Shelden or Shelton who moved with Iris to Lichfield before demob in 1946; and Gwen Proctor, who married a Sergeant Tinker from the stores.

Iris said there was always a WAAF officer in the office plus Warrant Officer Ron Mutton and Flight Sergeant Pat (Jacko) Jackson who was posted to the Far East in 1945-46. She has met Doris Harris and Ron Mutton on visits to England but has never traced Pat Jackson.

Iris recalls walking from The Hockett, through the orchard in Spring and seeing the blossom and the baby lambs, to The Jolly Farmer for a port and lemon with her favourite airman. On the way back, she had to climb over the stile in her tight WAAF skirt. On Sunday mornings she picked mushrooms for breakfast in a nearby field. "I can still taste them - real mushrooms". Iris loved drill and square-bashing and recalls marching to Cox Green when the top brass thought the WAAFs needed fresh air.

Iris was one of three WAAFs who flew on the AOG Anson service; Doris Harris and Marjory Brown were the others. Jim Mollison was the pilot on her last trip back from Scotland. "The sky was full of fighter planes taking off. The weather was not very good and all I can remember is seeing the tops of trees and telephone wires by the side of railway lines, all the way back to White Waltham, and cranking the undercarriage up and down."

The Hockett, Cookham Dean; the cross marks the spot where the tree was planted on VE-Day.

Iris was in the office when a Halifax bomber overshot the airfield and landed on the main GWR railway line. "We rushed out to hide behind a bunker as it had a bomb on board. The Canadian crew were badly injured. The bomb was safely removed but the trains were re-routed for three days while the plane was removed."

The RAF equipment section, based on the airfield, 1943. Second row from back, civilian on extreme right, Mr Nichol; in same row, second left, Beryl Smallwood (nee Waller); next row, second WAAF from left, Pamela Fletcher (nee Meekcoms); same row, fourth from right, Sgt Aggio; fifth from right, Sgt Tinkum; sitting, second from right, Ron Mutton; fourth from left, Pip Morgan; front row, extreme left, Jean Phipps.

On VE-Day (May 8, 1945), Iris was one of only three or four staff left at The Hockett; the others had gone to London. An Air Vice-Marshal, believed to be Sir Arthur Coningham, visited the house and planted a tree on the lawn which they christened with gin "My first experience with gin. Oh, my head," Iris comments.

Sir Arthur was head of the 2nd Tactical Air Force in Europe. He later became Air Officer Commanding-in-Chief of Flying Training Command from 1945-47 and died in January 1948. In Who Was Who 1941-50, his address is shown as The Hockett, Cookham Dean. Sadly, the tree has not survived.

In the 1980s, Iris contacted Ronald Hill, then living in Michigan, USA, who had worked for ATA for two years. He started as an office boy at £1 4s 6d (£1.25) a week. His father was ATA's chief accountant. Ronald reported to Flight Lieutenant Tugwell in the equipment section and later worked in the inspection department with Captain Macpherson and afterwards with Freddie Laker (now Sir Freddie) in the office of the chief engineer, Commander Cauthray. Ronald drew the posters for parties held at Altmore and elsewhere.

He lived in requisitioned quarters over the garages and stables of a large house near the Thames, beyond Winter Hill. He sometimes went on weekend flights as far as Prestwick in Scotland and flew many times in the AOG Anson, winding down the undercarriage by hand on the approach to landing. The day before D-Day (June 6, 1944), Ronald helped paint black and white stripes on aircraft and stencilled the Ferdinand the Bull mascot on Air Movement Flight Ansons.

# 9

## Paley Street Caries on

As I came out of Waltham Chapel after morning service on Sunday September 3, 1939, with my father, the late Mr John Bennett leaned over his gate at Brook House, Paley Street, and told us: "The war has started". The chapel would need blacking out, as it still held evening services. Shutters, on light wooden frames covered with tarred paper, were soon made for the chapel and the Chapel Hall across the road. Both are deserted now, but the hall was my centre of social life throughout the war.

Like other families, we had evacuees billeted on us - Eric and Laura Darwin from Paddington. They stayed only a few weeks. Much later in the war, in 1943, we had a Land Girl to lodge with us - Violet Banks, who worked at Sheepcote Farm, Paley Street, which was managed for Mrs Annie Skinner by her nephew, Ted Smith, organist at the chapel. Violet brought a breath of London to our home, Meadowside. My brothers and I had no sister and although we often used to tease Violet, we helped her wash her hair in rainwater, collected in a tank from off the house roof.

As the farm had no livestock, Violet was able to go home most weekends to Kingston-on-Thames. When she got back on Sunday evening, my brother John usually had several friends in to listen to records on the wind-up gramophone - Bing Crosby, the Mills Brothers, Flanagan and Allen and Glenn Miller among them.

John organised two variety concerts in the Chapel Hall in aid of the Red Cross Prisoners-of-War Fund. The first raised £60 and the second £75 - incredible sums for those days. Admission was 7½p and the hall held 100 people. Donations and raffles made up the balance. Multiply the pounds by at least ten for today's currency. Customs and Excise demanded payment of Entertainment Tax on the proceeds after the first concert but, by visiting the Customs officer in Henley-on-Thames, John was able to gain exemption from the tax as it was a charity event.

The Chapel Hall, lit by oil-lamps and heated by a coke stove, was formerly Boyne Hill Baptist Church. It was moved to Paley Street in 1932 and had been used for entertainments pre-war. John and his helpers extended the stage so that the piano could be accommodated and used control cables from an Avro Anson and pulleys so that the stage curtains could be operated from one side. I was allowed to operate the curtains at the second concert. One concert was repeated at Shottesbrooke Park for wounded Polish soldiers living there. My father, George Tomlinson, compered the concerts. I still remember one of my brother's wisecracks: "What you don't read in the local paper, can be heard in the Blue Bus". The Blue Bus was the service operated by Wests of Bray from Maidenhead to Paley Street via Bray, Holyport and Moneyrow Green. The single fare from Paley Street to Maidenhead was for years six old pence (2½p). During the war the company had two Bedford buses with wooden seats, similar to those used by the Forces. People who had seen the last house at the Rialto or Plaza cinema could catch the 10.15 p.m. service - the "picture bus". Games evening on Mondays at the Chapel Hall was like a youth club for an extended age range - 13 to 40 plus. We played billiards, snooker, darts, table tennis and draughts. Later in the war, an Italian prisoner from the Kimbers Lane camp, who used to come, proved unbeatable at draughts.

Most farms in the village had one Land Girl and German and Italian prisoners-of-war worked on the Land at various times. Their British battledress uniforms had large coloured patches on them but few ever attempted to escape. Paley Street was a better billet than the Russian Front.

My Uncle Walter's dairy farm in How Lane had to plough up part of its grassland to grow corn and I helped regularly in the summer. Loading (arranging) the sheaves on the horse-drawn waggons was my favourite job and I also learned to milk a cow by hand.

My brother John built an air-raid shelter in the garden but as the soil was heavy clay, it was always damp and we never used it. One night when we might have needed it was Saturday February 13, 1943, when an Armstrong-Whitworth Whitley bomber crashed in the Great Wood not far from the house now called Littlefield Farm and only 300-400 yards from my home.

I still have the schoolboy account I wrote of the crash at the time. One member of the crew was killed; he was the bomb aimer who was housed in the nose of the aircraft. The other four members of the crew were taken to Maidenhead Hospital; the rear gunner was safe in his turret in a tree top.

The crash happened at 10.45 p.m. My brother John put on his tin hat and Home Guard greatcoat and took his rifle. He had no ammunition but thought rattling the bolt might frighten the crew if they were Germans!

My cousin Horace from How Lane Farm, who was a St John Ambulance volunteer, gave first aid at the site of the crash and was on duty at Maidenhead Hospital when the crew were brought in later that night.

RAF White Waltham put men on to guard the plane and we took them tea and sandwiches next morning. Throughout the day, sightseers came to look at the crash. Dismantling of the aircraft started on Wednesday and by Saturday it had all been taken away. I had a piece of parachute silk as a souvenir.

Paley Street supported appeals for the war effort and my father had a scrap iron dump by our roadside hedge. Loads of three to four tons could be collected but it was many months before our small heap was cleared.

The Junior Dad's Army. Fortunately, they never had to fight the Hitler Youth. Back row, left to right: Roy Smith, Dennis Tomlinson, Bob Fleming. Front row, left to right, Eric Shepherd, Peter Golding, John French.

Although Paley Street had its own Post Office (now the Post House), which was also a grocer's and bakery, our family registered with Keeley Bros at Knowl Hill for rationed foods. They delivered weekly throughout the war. Very occasionally, they brought an extra packet of tea but otherwise we received only the official rations. Having a large garden and keeping hens meant that we were much better fed than people in towns.

Like all boys, my friends and I played soldiers with home-made wooden rifles. Our Junior Dad's Army - the How Lane and Littlefield Green Infantry - later became the Amalgamated Commando Corps so that we could wear ACC shoulder flashes on our "uniform". ACC was the Army Catering Corps and the shoulder flashes could be bought at L. J. Blackstone, a Maidenhead tailor.

Items dumped by American soldiers at their camp at Ascot Road, Holyport on part of what is now the Maidenhead by-pass, including gaiters, hats, stripes, badges and mess tins, added to our equipment. We had our own tests in aircraft recognition and our own handwritten magazine. We once held a night exercise in a large field at Sheepcote Lane and used a real thunderflash!

The Americans were in tents with white chimneys from their heating stoves sticking out of the top. After a German plane had dropped a few incendiaries on the camp, the chimneys were quickly repainted brown, so Andy Duncan, a former resident of Holyport, told me.

One other memory of the Americans has been mentioned by several people. Some white Americans were attending a dance at the New Hall, Waltham St Lawrence, but when a group of black Americans came in, the whites told them to leave. The black soldiers went to The Star pub and local people offered their sympathy.

Although it had no factories, the Paley Street end of the village housed the searchlight site at Drift Road (see Chapter 3). Opposite the searchlight site was a dummy airfield. It consisted of lights (at ground level) powered by a generator and switched on each night. The site was bombed once but no damage was done. Poles put up in a field were supposed to deter parachutists.

# 10

## Woodlands Park takes Shelter

People living at Woodlands Park were considered at greater risk of bombing or aircraft crashes because of their close proximity to the airfield. Regulations allowed shelters to be built for people living within 1000 yards of the aerodrome and expenditure of £2500 was agreed by Berkshire Emergency Committee for Civil Defence in December 1940 for the Woodlands Park shelters. Two were built in the field next to the then butcher's shop at Woodlands Park Corner, one in Breadcroft Road and another in the railway field at Breadcroft Lane.

Quentin Todd (see Chapter 4) recalls that gas masks were issued to Woodlands Park residents at Smiths the bakers. Concrete anti-tank blockades were built across Cannon Lane by the butcher's shop and were demolished after the war. They were an anti-invasion precaution. and narrowed the road so that only one vehicle could pass at a time.

Other anti-tank blockades were built on the railway bridge in Breadcroft Lane and are still there (1998). An Army camp was set up in the railway field for the purpose of guarding the airfield and another on the bridge in Breadcroft Lane.

Quentin's family took in two evacuees from London - Kathleen and Elsie - but they did not stay long. They then took in the Brett family and the Hornbys next door took in the Laidlaw family.

The weekly allowance for having an evacuee, paid by the Government, was 8s 6d (42p). Most evacuees returned to London before the war ended but others stayed on in the area after the war ended. The ten or so villages in the Cookham Rural District, which included White Waltham, accepted a total of 3000 evacuees.

When the local ARP (Air Raid Precautions) group was set up, Quentin was the youngest member at 16 or 17. The only other name he recalls is Mr Buck who lived in the last bungalow in Woodlands Park Road. He writes: "We used to meet in the Methodist Chapel once a week, but when there was an air raid over London or when the air raid siren sounded at night, the ARP met by the anti-tank blockades in Cannon Lane. We rarely turned out in the day."

In 1998, anti-tank blockades were still in place on Breadcroft Road railway bridge.

"An AFS (Auxiliary Fire Service) unit was formed. I recall Gordon Hopkins of Woodlands Park Road and Tommy Green from Cherry Garden Lane joining." (This was the unit at Waltham Place; other members were Gerald Ewers and Bill Watts. Its trailer pump was later acquired by ML Aviation then went to Maidenhead Fire Station and in 1979 was with Berkshire Fire Brigade at Crowthorne).*

Mr Frank Bissley, who often wrote to the Maidenhead Advertiser, signing himself F. Beaumont Bissley, was responsible for much of the housing development in Woodlands Park. He had a small farm with six cows in Highfield Lane, Cox Green. George Kirby, who worked for him, delivered milk straight from the churn carried on his trade bicycle to regular customers.

In spring and summer Mr Kirby would drive the cows along the road from Highfield Lane to the railway field each day. When Mr Bissley gave up the field post-war, it was taken over by Mr Charles Chick and Quentin Todd who ran it as a smallholding. Mr Chick was also the

*The Cut, Autumn 1979.

security sergeant at the Anti-Attrition factory entrance. They used the air raid shelter in the railway field to store hay and straw. A further indication of how rural Woodlands Park was is Quentin's recollection of the Thatched Cottage public house in Cannon Lane just pre-war. "It had an oak tree in the front and was run by Tommy Grimmett, a little old man who had to go down the steps to the cellar every time somebody wanted a pint or half-pint. The pub was still lit by oil lamps. At the beginning of the war, it was taken over by Frank and Daisy Barratt."

Quentin's list of shops will bring back memories to older Woodlands Park residents. The only name remaining from those days is Hammants whose garage was much smaller then. He recalls Smiths the bakers, now part of Hammants; the Post Office and newsagents run by the Frost family until 1939-40 and then taken over by Mr Frisby (newsagent) and Mr Duval (Post Office). The butcher's, originally Tom Morris, was taken over by a Mr Weller and later by Reg Lawrence, who served in the White Waltham Home Guard Platoon. Post-war, the garage of the butcher's became Vic Hatcher's fish shop.

Quentin Todd with his cows, taken in 1947.

There was Wallace's store, which later became a mini-mart, and a general store at the end of Breadcroft Lane owned by Mr Heaver and later taken over by the Harrisons. Opposite this shop was Wagner's Precast Concrete Works - the only light industry in Woodlands Park before the war. Where Willant Close now is there was a driveway leading to Yandall's nurseries and glasshouses.

With so many aircraft landing and taking off at the airfield, there were occasional tragedies. As well as being a ferry pool, White Waltham also ran an ATA flying school and the air movements flight, which ferried VIPs and others all over Great Britain.

One well-remembered incident was on March 15, 1942, when a Fairchild Argus, one of ATA's taxi aircraft, crashed on a bungalow at Smithfield Road. Three pilots died in the crash; only one, Third Officer Pamela Duncan survived. Charlie Gorrod, an ATA engineering inspector, went into the bungalow and was severely burned when the aircraft exploded. He received the British Empire Medal for his bravery.

Twenty-five civilians, including Quentin Todd's brother Derek, were injured. Fred Clements, who wrote about the crash in the Spring 1980 issue of the local magazine, The Cut, spent three months in Cliveden Hospital having been severely burned. He received a letter of appreciation from Gerard d'Erlanger, head of ATA. A full account of the crash appears in the second edition of "A Quiet War", published by Cox Green Local History Group.

This photograph of the VE-Day party held at Woodlands Park Methodist Church was supplied by Vera Venables (nee Luck). Back row, left to right: Mr Wheeler, Jean Gilmore, Jean Mears, David Sherwood, Sylvia Clipsham, Winnie Tegg, June Samways, Ron Clipsham. Middle row: left to right, Betty Gilmore, Sylvia Bird, Vera Luck, Ada Luck, Bill Kierley, David Gilmore, Vic Burton. Front row; left to right: Vera Clayton, Kenny James, Pam Gilmore, John Tegg.

# 11

## The RAF Moves In

Though the RAF dominated the village throughout the war, it was the Army who were the first arrivals.

Quentin Todd (Chapter 10) recalls soldiers coming to Woodlands Park and Ann Aiken (nee Wells), who was living in Butchers Lane, told me that they were Territorials who by then would have been mobilised. The Cookham Rural District Rates Book for 1939-40 shows White Waltham House, the former home of Lady Brownrigg, in the ownership of the 6th Battalion, Royal Berkshire Regiment, from November 1939.

But the Army's stay was short-lived and White Waltham House and The Grove, listed as Air Ministry property from December 1939, were occupied by the RAF. The Smithy House, home of the Carlisles and until the 1920s, the Horse and Groom public house, later became the RAF officers' mess. Mrs Carlisle was company commander of the 3rd Berkshire Company Maidenhead Unit of the ATS (Auxiliary Territorial Service) and her name appeared in advertisements for volunteers. (The ATS were the women soldiers who served with the Army both at home and overseas). The RAF's main camp was behind The Grove. Wooden huts were also put up in land on the opposite corner to The Grove which Sir John Smith of Shottesbrooke Park later bought from the Ministry and gave to the Parish Council as a public open space.

Further huts were built on the edge of Shottesbrooke Park, not far from the officers' mess. It was close to these huts that a Short Stirling crashed on October 22, 1943. It is thought to have been struck by lightning. (See "A Quiet War", 2nd Edition, published by Cox Green Local History Group for a fuller account).

Although sited so close to the airfield, the RAF station was not part of the airfield's activities. From 1941-42, RAF White Waltham was a Signal

Pool and from 1943-45, a WT (Wireless Telegraphy) Exercise Camp. Records at the Public Record Office show many movements of men, equipment and vehicles. The Wireless Unit Formation Section was moved from Putteridge Bury near Luton, to White Waltham in October 1942. From October 21-24, 1942, 1000 cases of equipment were loaded and dispatched by rail to ports of embarkation and 95 motor vehicles with WT gear went in convoy by road to ports of embarkation.

The Grove House - the new office building which has replaced the house which stood at the top of Cherry Garden Lane and was occupied by the RAF for many years. The main camp was located behind the old house.

In April 1943, 1100 personnel left White Waltham for RAF Chigwell in Essex. Chigwell, a former barrage balloon centre, was to be the country's main base for the formation, equipping and final training of Mobile Signals Units. The Mobile Signals Units would be needed for "air traffic control" of military aircraft in campaigns across Europe and in the Far East.

From April 1943, RAF White Waltham worked closely with Chigwell and became a sub-unit of that station. Both were part of the RAF's No 26 Signals Group whose headquarters was at Langley Hall, Slough.

In June 1942, RAF White Waltham had become the parent station for RAF Regiment men based on the airfield. But they were not responsible for the RAF Equipment Section serving the ATA (see Chapter 8).

A NAAFI (Navy, Army and Air Force Institutes) canteen was built for the RAF on land adjoining The Grove and opposite Bury Court Farm. Dances were held there which civilians (men and women) could attend. In addition to the NAAFI, there was also a civilian canteen, run by volunteers in a barn close to White Waltham Church. Organiser of the Barn Canteen was Mrs Margaret Creese from Paley Street and among her helpers were May Golding, Grace Winchcombe and her sister Vera Wale who, on marriage, became Vera Reading. Grace's daughter Doreen also helped occasionally. Doreen's father, Fred Winchcombe, was an ATA policeman, often on duty at the Waltham Road entrance to the airfield.

Doreen and her husband, Bert Griffiths, met while he was stationed at The Manor House, Paley Street. He was in the Royal Artillery attached to the RAF at The Grove. Bert, who was from North Wales, had been called up in July 1939 and served as an observer with the Royal Artillery's Searchlight Unit, attached to the RAF. He was in White Waltham from September 1940 and after a few weeks at The Manor House, moved to The Grove to prepare for embarkation to South Africa in January 1941. He eventually transferred to the RAF in Beirut in 1942.

The former blacksmith's shop which stood at the side of the Officers' Mess. It was occupied by Braemar Antiques until early 1997.

Like other RAF men who married girls from the village, Bert stayed in the area and he and Doreen celebrated their golden wedding in 1997. The Manor House was later the home of Senior Commander Philip Wills, second-in-command of ATA.

A number of RAF men who were stationed in the village have given me their reminiscences. John Taylor, a native of Norwich, has only one memory of White Waltham: "It was bitterly cold". He was there from January-March, 1943, sleeping in a tent. He was posted from Northern Ireland with hundreds of others. They were in Blue Group which was to become the 2nd Tactical Air Force. He was a wireless operator and served with a mobile radar unit in France, Belgium, Holland and Germany.

The former Officers' Mess, which is now divided into five private houses. Donald Peek, who was stationed at White Waltham from 1953-55 and worked in the bar, describes the Officers' Mess as follows: "Going through the main entrance in the older part, there was a small ante-room with the bar on the left of the ante-room. Off the older part there were temporary buildings which consisted of a very large ante-room, used for various functions, including summer and winter balls. To the left of the large ante-room were the kitchens, beyond that a very large dining room. The only officers who lived in the older part of the Mess were two or three very senior officers." During his six months as barman, Donald lived in the loft in the old part which contained two RAF-type beds, a couple of lockers and a table. The window looked out over the rear of the old building. Most officers lived in huts in the grounds of the Officers' Mess. Donald recalls a carol service he attended in White Waltham Church, with all ranks present. He sang in a mixed choir of airmen and airwomen. The lessons were read by officers and Senior NCOs (Non-commissioned Officers).

John Yarnold, a wireless operator from Wallasey, Cheshire, calls White Waltham the best station in his RAF career. During his time, in the middle years of the war, the wireless operators were mostly WAAFs and the men watched transmitters or supervised the watches. He was supervising the transmitters one hot evening in an articulated vehicle in the middle of a field. He left the door open and, unknown to him, a kitten crept in and hid under one of the transmitters. Later there was a bang and one of the sets stopped; the kitten had got too close to one of the valves and been electrocuted.

A happier experience for John was when he was coming off duty early one morning and picked two roses from the garden at White Waltham House. Later that day he was meeting his fiancee at Euston Station. When challenged by two Service Policemen, at the barrier, he had no pass. So he pointed to the roses on his fiancee's coat and said "Just Married". The bluff worked.

John took part in entertainments on the camp and painted scenery and banners and once did a song and dance act in Maidenhead Town Hall, with a pal, both dressed as WAAFs, about personnel on the camp. He cycled to other villages and attended dances in the New Hall, Waltham St Lawrence. He once spent a week in Cliveden Hospital and was visited by Nancy, Lady Astor. His wife's wedding ring was bought at Biggs, the Maidenhead jewellers.

One advantage of being close to the airfield was that airmen could sometimes get a lift in an ATA plane. John Yarnold went in a Wellington bomber bound for Hawarden, near Chester, but a violent thunderstorm forced it to land at an airfield near Newcastle-under-Lyme. He hitchhiked by road for the rest of the journey.

Someone else who enjoyed RAF White Waltham was WAAF Corporal Dorothy Hurst, also a wireless operator. She is now Dorothy Reid. She writes: "My first introduction to White Waltham was one summer afternoon in time for tea. We sat down at a small table, about six WAAFs in the middle of a very large hangar, filled with the RAF. Next day we were moved to a smaller one which was more peaceful.

Hut 4 on the main RAF camp site, with the airfield perimeter road running by the side. Donald Peek lived in this hut for part of his time at White Waltham. At one point during the war, accommodation was so tight that 50 airmen slept in the hangar on the relief landing ground at Waltham St Lawrence and cycled en masse to White Waltham.

The village seemed to have been taken over by the RAF. There were very few WAAFs when I first went there, but more arrived as time went by.

I did my wireless operating in a small trailer situated in the corner of a field, halfway between the camp and White Waltham House, going up towards the house on the left-hand side.

There were about six or eight operators to a watch with a Sergeant (RAF) superintendent in charge. It was a four-watch system and I remember the night watch being fun. We were able to collect rations from the cookhouse and cook our suppers in the trailer. It was quite busy, passing and receiving messages with a great deal of interference".

Dorothy used the Barn Canteen and also The Beehive public house. "In the evenings the pub was packed - not only Service people but civilians as well. All seemed to get on well together", she says. She also visited the dances at the New Hall.

"I enjoyed my time at White Waltham very much. I had old family friends living in Maidenhead, so a lot of my off-duty times were spent with them". Her memory of the village is as "a delightful country place with lanes and fields".

Wally Yates-Cotterell was at White Waltham as a Corporal wireless operator from March 1944 to September 1945. He writes: "Together with other Head Office signals staff, we maintained 24-hour continuous wireless communication with a number of Mobile Signals Units. This was part of their training before being posted overseas.

"I married a lady from Cheshire in August 1944 and working shifts gave me the opportunity to be away from camp more frequently than if I had had a day job. Many times I would come off night duty, phone the ATA office at the airfield to enquire if there was a plane going to Cheshire, and if so, could I hitch-hike a lift. One occasion I was flying north, but flying west to east was the air armada of troop carriers and planes towing gliders for the devastating battle at Arnhem in Holland".

The tall building in the centre was part of the RAF's MT (Motor Transport) section on the site of what is now White Waltham Garage.

# 12

## All Set for D-Day

Ray Loveland served in the RAF as a wireless mechanic from January 1940 to August 1943 when he was commissioned as a signals officer. He was demobbed in March 1946. He has given this detailed account of his time at White Waltham.

"To support the 2nd Tactical Air Force for the invasion of Normandy, a number of different types of Mobile Signals Units were formed. These ranged from tiny units consisting of a corporal and two airmen to large units with six officers and many NCOs and airmen. These units were formed and trained at RAF Chigwell in Essex. White Waltham was used as base for some of these units after training and there were a few signals personnel stationed there permanently. The commanding officer was Squadron Leader Dellbridge and the station signals officer was Flight Lieutenant Noble.

Most of the Mobile Signals Units were equipped with their own transport so that they could be deployed by boarding landing ships. In addition some units were formed which were intended to provide rapid emergency back-up for any airfields established in Normandy which had their signals equipment put out of use by enemy action.

These units had no transport of their own, all the equipment being mounted in crates for rapid deployment by air (in Dakotas). These units were known as ATSU's (Air Transportable Signals Units). Four of these units were stationed at White Waltham early in May 1944 in readiness for the D-Day assault, the airfield there being ideal for the type of operation intended.

These units consisted of a signals officer, a cypher officer and 12 NCOs and airmen.

The four units were:

    No 1 ATSU (CO* Flying Officer E.H. Griffiths)
    No 2 ATSU (CO Flying Officer R.A. Loveland)
    No 3 ATSU (CO Flying Officer J. Chapman)
    No 4 ATSU (CO Flying Officer N. Powell)

The officers' mess was in the former pub at the end of the village and airmen were accommodated in Nissen huts on the opposite side of the road. Our equipment was stored in Nissen huts in Butchers Lane, opposite the council houses. The officers' mess was very comfortable and had a full-size billiards table. I spent much off-duty time there playing snooker.

As with other units awaiting D-Day, security was tight, with all personnel confined to camp. D-Day (June 6, 1944) came and we just sat and waited. After about a week, No 1 ATSU was ordered to Portsmouth, not by air, but by road to join a convoy to Normandy. The unit duly departed. We had no definite news of them but many rumours were circulating including one saying that they had all been lost at sea. About 48 hours after leaving, they returned to White Waltham intact and unharmed.

They had waited at Portsmouth for shipment by the Navy who apparently failed to allocate a space in a landing ship in time for the rendezvous in Normandy. Owing to the delay, the need for their services in France no longer existed and they were ordered back to base. This was the only piece of 'action' the ATSUs saw and we continued to stand by at White Waltham. It was a very frustrating experience as we were all confined to camp with nothing to do except occasionally check our equipment. After a while, the position was eased with only two units being on stand-by at a time. Personnel were able to leave camp for a few hours on some days.

The RAF personnel, led by the CO, Squadron Leader Dellbridge, integrated with the village - so much so that events were organised with airmen and villagers taking part. I well remember the CO entering a team for the local tug-of-war competition from the officers' mess.

There were only about a dozen officers in the mess and as eight were needed for the team, this left very little choice. The team selected proved totally unsuitable and a team of locals completely overwhelmed us.

* Commanding Officer

A great day arrived in late August when a combined village/RAF fête was organised. Various events took place during the day - I took part in a cricket match - and it culminated with a dance at the NAAFI. This was going in great style when, at about 10 p.m., the Station CO called the officers of the ATSUs together and said he had just been told that our units were to join the First Allied Airborne Army the next day for possible deployment in the advance from Northern France into Belgium.

He told us that we were to be at the Allied Airborne Army HQ at Sunninghill Park, Ascot, by 9 a.m. next day. This would entail loading 12 three-ton lorries which were due to arrive at 6 a.m. and then drive to Sunninghill Park - no great distance, but that was the least of our problems.

We had to round up the NCOs and airmen who were enjoying themselves in various ways at the dance, get them bedded down in the huts and ensure they were up at first light to load up. Some of the officers had invited their wives and girl friends to the fête and they were accommodated in the officers' mess. Many hasty farewells were said next morning.

We more or less completed the timetable which had been set for us and were only 30 minutes late arriving at Sunninghill Park - in all the circumstances, a considerable achievement.

Our stay at Sunninghill Park was almost a repeat of our time at White Waltham, as again our services were not required. A redeeming feature was that we enjoyed American messing which was vastly superior to anything the RAF could provide. As the ATSUs were never used, it was decided that they were to be disbanded and we returned to White Waltham in December (1944) to break up the units. All personnel returned to RAF Chigwell and were posted to other Mobile Signals Units. I ended up taking a completely different type of unit to Germany in March 1945".


*Postscript. Ann Aiken (see Chapter 5) remembers attending the fete and winning a comb on one of the stalls. "I was quite pleased as it was something you couldn't buy then," Ann writes. The reason, of course, was war-time shortages which affected almost everything that people wished to buy.*

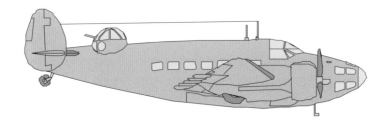

Lockheed Hudson

# 13

## Past and Present

The war ended for my family when my brother Brian came home at 6.30 a.m. on VJ-Day - August 15, 1945. He told us that Japan had surrendered, following the dropping of two atomic bombs on Hiroshima and Nagasaki, and that the war was over. He had been abroad for four years and served with the 8th Army in Egypt, Sicily and Italy. Ten days later he married his fiancee, Kay Johnson, in White Waltham Church; he still had two more years to serve in the Army.

The rundown of ATA had already begun by this time. An air pageant was held in September and on November 30, 1945, the last ATA Anson landed at White Waltham. My brother John filled in with temporary work at Hammants Garage until called up in the Fleet Air Arm; his friend Ken Golding went fruit picking until called up in the RAF. Both had been made redundant well before ATA's closedown.

Fairey Aviation were the main occupants of the airfield from 1947, test-flying the Firefly Mark 8 and the Gannet prototype and carrying out final assembly of aircraft built at the Hayes factory. Their unconventional Gyrodyne and Rotodyne flew from the airfield. Fairey Air Surveys operated from the site. The Duke of Edinburgh and Prince Charles learned to fly there. Oakfield, the Ewers' family home (see Chapter 2) was demolished in 1953.

The RAF stayed in the village until 1973 and had a variety of units based on the airfield. Married quarters were built for officers and airmen. Altmore, the house on Cherry Garden Lane, was used as officers' married quarters for a time and later as airmen's married quarters.

The RAF station was Headquarters Reserve Command which later became Home Command. The following information is based on a chapter in the book Home Commands of the Royal Air Force since 1915, by Denis C. Bateman:

> The original Reserve Command, formed at Hendon on February 1, 1939, moved to White Waltham a month later. It was disbanded on May 27, 1940, and reformed in London on May 1, 1946, at Alexandra and Imperial Houses, Air Ministry, Kingsway, before moving back to White Waltham on October 7, 1946. Home Command, as it had then become, was finally disbanded on April 1, 1959.

The West London Aero Club, formed by ATA pilots at the end of the war, still flourishes. It adopted ATA's motto, "Aetheris Avidi", (Eager for the Air) and its premises are the former ATA administration block, moved from its old site to the Waltham Road side of the airfield. The airfield is currently home to approximately 150 light aircraft.

Altmore, the house in Cherry Garden Lane used by RAF Reserve pilots pre-war and by ATA throughout the war.

The main hangars on the railway side of the airfield were demolished a few years ago and the site is now Maidenhead Office Park. The old Cherry Garden Lane railway bridge was demolished and a new bridge built with a new road, Westacott Way, to give access to the Office Park.

Mrs Cook's Restawhile Café in Cherry Garden Lane, famed for its bread pudding, has gone. The 'Coach and Horses', favourite pub of ATA pilots, run by Bill and Madge Sweetzer, is now 'The Shire Horse'. Altmore House, mentioned by Group Captain Alan Deere in his autobiography Nine Lives, published by Hodder and Stoughton, is now divided into flats. Altmore was the mess for trainee RAF pilots when Alan Deere arrived there in 1937.

In the centre of the village, the only sign of the RAF's occupation is part of one of the MT (Motor Transport) Section's buildings which is on the site of White Waltham Garage. The former officers' mess has been divided into five houses and the blacksmith's shop close by, run for many years by Charlie Herbert, has long since closed.

West London Aero Club's buildings were formerly ATA's administration block.

Several new houses stand on the site of White Waltham House - one preserving the name White Waltham House. On the opposite side of the road, White Waltham Cricket Club has a new pavilion. The village school has been extended and has seven teachers and 160 pupils compared with four teachers and 100 pupils when I was there. The village post office and bakery have closed, and the Barn Canteen is now a private house.

The Grove House, usually known affectionately as The Grove, stood empty after the RAF left and eventually became derelict. The new office block built on the site in 1989-90 is named Grove House and in 1997 the occupants were Newbridge Networks Ltd., a Canadian corporation whose business is computer networking.

The main occupant of Maidenhead Office Park, mentioned earlier, is

Nortel, a leading global provider of digital network solutions who work with customers in more than 150 countries to design, build and integrate their communications and advanced digital networks. In 1998, Nortel were occupying three linked buildings, housing 800 staff, with two other buildings under construction to house a further 450.

As mentioned in Chapter 5, the Anti-Attrition factory site is now Foundation Park. Seven new buildings have gone up on the former ML Aviation site which now takes in the area where the NAAFI stood; the largest of these is occupied by Newland Engineering, which manufactures gearboxes and transmission components for racing cars.

Maidenhead Office Park, built on the site of the original hangar on the railway side of White Waltham airfield. A new road from the A4, Westacott Way, gives access to the site.

The view along Waltham Road today is very different from that seen by SAC (Senior Aircraftman) Tony Watton on his arrival in 1964. He noticed a World War I Fokker triplane on the airfield and wondered just what he was coming to. He later discovered that this was one of the replicas built by the late Doug Bianchi's Personal Plane Services for the film Those Magnificent Men in Their Flying Machines.

Tony, who worked in the officers' mess, describes his three years at White Waltham as "the most wonderful years of my life" and the village as "the most beautiful place on earth."

Of all the recollections I received in compiling this book there was one which gave a link with the Victorian era. It was from Ann Aiken (see

Chapter 5) and describes two people I remember well - Miss Lee and Mrs Ferguson who lived at Albert Cottage (now renamed Chimneys). Ann writes: "They still dressed in the Victorian style: long black skirts, white blouses, very tiny waists, boots and black hats. We sometimes used to see them go across to the shop. It seemed as if time had stood still for them." Their mother, who had kept the Beehive many years before, used to read the Bible to the men in the tap-room on Sunday evenings.

The West London Aero Club preserves ATA's motto - Aetheris Avidi, Eager for the Air.

White Waltham has moved on and changed. There is more industry here than in the peak days of 1940-45 when local people were trained in new skills to meet the exacting requirements of war production. However, I hope this book will help the past to live and help a future generation to understand the significant contribution White Waltham made to the Second World War.

The past came alive for me in June 1997. I had driven down what remains of the White Waltham end of Cherry Garden Lane - past where the RAF camp used to be. As I stepped out of the car, six Tiger Moths flew over - the type of aircraft which was the first to fly from the airfield 62 years previously.

*Epilogue. In July 1998, I spoke to East Harling Women's Institute in Norfolk. One of the members told me she had worked at the airframe factory at Speke, near Liverpool. This factory was, in 1937, intended for White Waltham but, due to strong local opposition, was not built there. The WI member worked 12 hours a day for seven days and then had a day off. She once had the chance to go inside a completed aircraft, a Bristol Blenheim, pressed a button marked "press" and the bomb doors opened to deposit the foreman on the floor below.*

TAILPIECE. Violet Banks (who later married Michael Shaw) has added to her experiences in the Women's Land Army (see page 49). Although there were no cows to be milked at Sheepcote Farm, there were steers (beef animals) to be brought in and fed. Violet also took horses to be shod by Charlie Herbert, the village blacksmith. One was nicknamed Deadlegs (because he was so slow) by her workmate, Charlie (Squitch) Williams. The other was a Percheron, named 'Punch', an ex-Army horse from the First World War. Violet, being short, needed help to get on the horse to ride the mile to the blacksmith's, but coming back, she walked rather than try to scramble up unaided.

The new building which has gone up on the former ML Aviation site.

# LIST OF BOOKS WHICH INCLUDE REFERENCES TO AIR TRANSPORT AUXILIARY

BRIEF GLORY
The Story of Air Transport Auxiliary.
By E.C. Cheesman (Air Transport Auxiliary Association)

AIR TRANSPORT AUXILIARY with cartoon illustrations

I COULDN'T CARE LESS.
By Anthony Phelps. (Harborough Publishing Co.)

THE FORGOTTEN PILOTS. By Lettice Curtis. (Foulis)

FLY AND DELIVER. By Hugh Bergel (Airlife)

WOMAN PILOT. By 'Jackie' Moggridge (Pan)

GOLDEN WINGS. By Alison King (White Lion Publishers)

WAAF WITH WINGS. By Y.M. Lucas (GMS Enterprises)

FLYING WARTIME AIRCRAFT.
By Hugh Bergel (David and Charles)

SPREADING MY WINGS.
By Diana Barnato Walker. (Patrick Stephens)

A.T.A. GIRL. By Rosemary du Cros. (Muller)

A HARVEST OF MEMORIES.
By Michael Fahie - a biography of Pauline Gower. (GMS Enterprises)

ATA Pilot's REMINDER BOOK. By Chief Technical Officer, ATA.

THE SKY AND I. By Veronica Volkersz. (W.H. Allen)

AMY JOHNSON. By C. Babbington Smith. (White)

MOUNT UP WITH WINGS. By Mary de Bunsen. (Hutchinson)

FERRY PILOT'S NOTES. (The small looseleaf 'bible' which ATA pilots carried. Contains notes on most types likely to be flown).

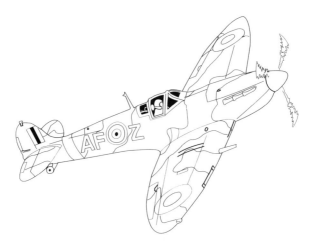

Supermarine Spitfire

# Appendix I

# Spitfire Ia – 'The Best Thing I Ever Flew'

ANN WOOD-KELLY arrived in England from USA in May 1942 to work as a pilot with ATA. She was only 20 and already had 350 flying hours to her credit, having trained in America under the Civilian Pilot Training Programme. She ferried 75 different types of aircraft with ATA, including 25 marks of the Spitfire, and was still flying in the summer of 2002.

Ann has presented the diary she kept of her first 14 months in England to Maidenhead Heritage Centre and has given the author permission to use extracts from it. It covers her training at Luton and at White Waltham and her time as a ferry pilot at No 6 Ferry Pool at Ratcliffe, Leicestershire - the prewar private airstrip of Sir Lindsay Everard. Some of the pilots, including Ann, lived in Ratcliffe Hall with Sir Lindsay and Lady Everard. She went frequently to London to meet friends.

Her diary describes how Ann, who was then Ann Wood, left in convoy from Canada in a Free French vessel. Sailing up the Mersey into Liverpool she passed the barrrage balloons attached to boats and buoys, saw bomb-damaged buildings and noticed the little red telephone boxes, which were new to her.

She travelled to London and arrived at White Waltham on May 27. A girl in a camouflaged car met her at Maidenhead railway station: 'We drove through sweet village parts and on to magnificent country. ATA has taken over many homes surrounding the airport and we were led to Captain Stokes in one such little red brick house with gardens and flowers all around.'

In London she was measured for her uniform at Austin Reed's, had lunch with a friend at the Savoy Hotel and then took the train to Luton

Airport - home of ATA's Elementary Flying School. Ann was billeted in the town. Her comment on the food: 'We eat aplenty but it is all starchy and a bit samey.' She notes that 'people line up here patiently in queues and one dutifully waits one's turn to mount the bus - all of which is a good contrast to the great pushing racket at home.'

On one of her many trips to London she notes that all the balloon barrages are up 'as they vaguely suspect a reprisal for last night's RAF attack on Cologne of over 1000 bombers.' She notes: 'Somehow these jaunts to London fill me with utter glee.'

During training she learns there are over 800 airfields in Britain. 'On the whole, things seem extremely well organised, which is rather comforting as there are innumerable hazards and the unpredictable weather.' By June 4, she is doing four hours flying a day plus ground training including Morse Code. She buys a women's bicycle for £10. On June 9 her first solo flight is in a Puss Moth.

June 17: 'Had cross-country check with Mrs Ebbage as I am having trouble with navigation. The maps are so different and every road and wood is supposed to mean something... Tried flying at 200 feet which is much better for then one can actually see the roads and the rises (hills) which are all clearly marked on the map.' (ATA pilots had no radio contact with the ground, hence the need for expert navigational skills). On June 23 she goes solo in the Hawker Hart. Another niggle over English food: 'Won't want to see cheese sandwiches again as long as I live.'

On transfer to the ferry flight a day is spent reading orders and being issued with rail vouchers (to exchange for tickets). Ann is given a float of £10 in case she is stuck out all night (after ferrying a plane). There are 'riotous' helpful hints on conduct on landing at an RAF aerodrome. 'Sometimes I wonder if the English have any sense of humour. They suggest that one deposits gum on the banister outside of mess halls - and takes care not to spit in the presence of the Commanding Officer.'

On June 27, Ann did two cross-country flights and landed at Sywell and White Waltham. 'It is lots of fun jazzing about and putting in at various fields. All watch office people are so very nice to you and one learns so much and sees such a lot that is totally new and different.' July 5: 'Wore my uniform for the first time. Like it very much but like best the USA on the sleeve.' July 9: 'Did a bit of Morse - it is actually driving me loco; can't seem to get it. Captain Hayden checked me out on Fairchilds. They are lovely to fly - so comfortable.' (The Fairchild was widely used as a taxi aircraft by ATA).

Her first ferry job was from Hullavington to South Cerney, having first had lunch in the officers' mess at Hullavington. She went back to White Waltham on July 21 and was billeted with other women pilots at Woolley Grange (also known as Woolley Firs), with Mr and Mrs Halliday. She is very critical of a former Air Vice-Marshal who came to dinner and was trying to get a billet further from the aerodrome so that he would qualify for a petrol ration. 'Am sure the men who sail in tankers would be pleased with his comments.'

Ann thought her technical instructor, a Mr Hall, mighty nice but complained that the canteen was an utter and complete mess. 'Believe I'll skip it and concentrate on breakfast and dinner at Woolley Grange.' She describes going to a gala cocktail party at a little drinking club on the Main Road.

On discovering that the censors sometimes return to ATA copies of personal letters written home, and that they are placed with the individual's records, Ann is concerned. 'I am continually comparing war efforts - describing personages - and commenting on some, both good and bad.' She fears this could prejudice others against her and make her chances and life in general far less pleasant.

But she enjoys walking through the 'stately home of England' grounds each morning on the way to the aerodrome. On July 25 she went to Skindles Hotel with three others and took a two-hour boat trip up the Thames, price 15 shillings per hour. 'It was fun. The river was very narrow and jammed with boats, many people having their supper in true English style.' Back at Skindles, they found the hotel jammed with

*Ann Wood-Kelly in ATA uniform*

merry-makers so crossed the river and had a delicious supper of ham, eggs and chips.

Next day she went to the club after dinner: 'Joan Hughes arrived and we chatted until midnight.' In London on July 27, she had her first air raid at 2am: 'Believe me, it is an eerie feeling - marvel how people stood it for months on end.' Next day was exam day. 'Wrote continually all day on carburettors, superchargers, fuels and fuel-air ratios. Superchargers I was definitely hazy on but all else was OK.' (The club was the American Club, later known as the All Services Club, on the corner of Bridge Road and Oldfield Road, Maidenhead. Prewar it was The Showboat night club and postwar it was the location of Optical Measuring Tools and later, Selbach and Whiting).

Back at White Waltham, she writes: 'White Waltham is an utter madhouse. Have never seen so many pilots seemingly doing nothing. But who am I to judge? See more Americans daily.' Commenting on a crash in which a student pilot was killed, she says: 'It takes just such a thing to pull us up by our bootstraps and make us wonder if we're next.'

Ann is reported to the CO for failing to wear her hat. She arrives at the club at 6.30pm: 'It is most attractive, lovely swimming pool... Winant's representative (John G. Winant was the US ambassador to Britain) arriving at 7pm. All speakers, including d'Erlanger, were poor - had fun gorging on ice cream. Spoke on BBC - answered dumb questions but it will be fun for mother if she hears it.'

Bank Holiday Monday: 'Everybody going somewhere. Have never seen such masses queuing for trains, trams, buses etc. Saw Fred Astaire in Holiday Inn... paid eight shillings (40p) which is colossal. Spent next day in and around a Harvard, doing type technical exam... Got my wings sewn on at long last.'

'Our little frictions (with other girl pilots) are just like a boarding school... I hope by some fate of Providence to keep on reasonably good terms with all, whenever possible. Time will tell.' August 6: 'Went off solo in Harvard. Landings not something to dream about but then perhaps they will come. Sometimes wonder when I start in a new ship (aircraft) how I ever started in this racket as it does take all I've got and then don't seem to catch as quickly as some others to new types. At least, it is always an effort for me.'

August 15: 'Weather really good. Got up early and cycled to 7.30am Mass - Feast of the Assumption. Rather big night on supposedly, as boys from Aldermaston (then a US Army Air Force base) are coming over. We all went to American Club.' August 24: 'Fixed supper - large glass of milk with ice. Next week it is rationed - three pints (per person) per week.'

She completed the required two hours in a Hurricane on August 27. Next day Captain Watson took her on an Oxford - 'that is all I lack to complete Training School.' Ferrying then began in earnest - in three days she had flown a Fairchild to Whitchurch, a Master to Kirkbride, a Martinet from Reading to Kirkbride and a Proctor coming south.

*Ann in her favourite aircraft - the Spitfire.*

Hearing that an American pilot had got rather lost, Ann comments: 'Was much relieved to know that others, even after much experience, can still get lost. It really takes solid concentration to navigate unless you are a native, for if you let yourself lapse a minute you are apt to be a gonner.' September 11: 'Got my first Hurricane to deliver from Langley. How those Anson pilots weave in and out between the balloon barrages is more than I know. Had trouble with the undercarriage and couldn't get it up, but all (came right) in time. So hazy that I followed the railroad to Kemble.'

On leave on Sunday September 13, she went to 8.30am Mass. In the evening rode her motor bike to Hurley for dinner at the Old Bell and heard Jimmy Mollison (Amy Johnson's ex-husband) talking to an Air

Vice-Marshal about something the AVM had said about Amy in India. The journey back was her first blackout ride - 'you can't see a thing and we had to push it up hills.' Boating on Thames and tea at Skindles next day.

September 17: 'Another nice job - Langley to Kemble in a Hurricane. Arrived about noon and spent rest of day taxiing around in an Anson - went to Llandow and St Athan.' September 22: 'Opened an account at Lloyds Bank. Tried to have radio cord fixed but no luck. Very poor service in Maidenhead. All shopkeepers much too busy to be nice about refusing work. My shoes were at menders two weeks but hadn't been touched... Got motor bike going and went for short trip to Bray, Windsor and Eton. Such fun seeing boys dressed in top hats etc. and watching them play on the playing fields of Eton, having heard so much about same. Get a bang out of that and wouldn't change my present lot for the world. Took Helen to Marlow and Henley for cocktails... Met Avery at the Riviera and dined at Sunny's' (Both in Maidenhead - the Riviera Hotel, close to Maidenhead Bridge, and Sunny's Club, a prewar night club close to the river in what looked like a private house).

*Skindles Hotel, where Ann went for tea.*

On September 23, Ann was back at Ratcliffe on a three-week secondment. She describes her billet, at Birstall, near Leicester: 'My room is tiny but adequate. The John is outside which must freeze you in the winter but there is a nice bath upstairs. Honestly believe that if there is an inconvenient or difficult way of doing something, the English will think of it.' September 24: 'Got terrific thrill out of exploring a new city (Leicester). The USA on my arm causes no end of comment. Think it good advertisement for it does publicise fact that we are in this as well.'

October 6: 'Big day. Had my first Spitfire from Castle Bromwich... The test pilot went over all details with us. It seemed quite straightforward, biggest snag being that engine heats up terribly and once you have started you have to hurry up all checks and taxiing and get in the sky... Arrived Kirkbride in 1 hour 10 minutes; had Master from there to Watton so had lovely day.'

On October 15, Ann was posted to Ratcliffe. October 21: 'Got my first ride in a Wimpey (Vickers Wellington). Never seen so many gadgets in one aircraft in all my life.' Next day she was the first 'gal' to fly a Fairey Swordfish from the Blackburn factory. October 24: 'I was stooge in a Stirling with Captain Chambers. He let me fly it to Oakington. They are monsters of the sky but handle beautifully and are extremely gentle in the air. Vaguely wondered if I would ever reach Class 5 (four-engined types)'. (The stooge was the second member of crew carried on four-engined aircraft to lower the undercarriage if the normal and reserve methods failed.)

Ann was at White Waltham on October 26 for the visit of Eleanor Roosevelt, wife of the American president, and Mrs Churchill, wife of Winston Churchill, the Prime Minister. 'At 9.30am all the gals, English and American, assembled in the Pilots' Rest Room. Pauline (Gower) read the programme. I was assigned to stand beside a Master. All the School's aircraft were lined up on the tarmac, so many women standing in front of each. Eleanor arrived promptly at 10. We all dashed from hangar out to our respective places. It was a complete downpour. She first went to the operations room and then passed by each plane, chatting to us as she went... Found her far more charming and appealing than I had thought - her face seemed soft and kindly. Mrs Churchill, very cute, was always getting lost in the crowd. There was brief speech-making in the hangar with a flag-draped Hudson for the background, then on to the mess which was jammed with good things.' Later the air raid siren sounded. 'We were all told to make for the (air raid) shelter. We went into the damp, cold places; it was rather a weird awakening and my first (time) in the shelter. I couldn't help but marvel at the German timing. Whether real or accidental, it struck rather forcibly.' (There was no air raid).

On November 9, Ann crashed a Spitfire at St Merryn in Cornwall and was off flying until November 19. She records going to Mass at Farm Street Church in London on Sunday November 15 and then cycling to Westminster Abbey for the bell-ringing service. (Church bells, which were to be the signal if a German invasion was taking place, had been silent since the beginning of the war but they were allowed to be rung throughout Britain on that day to celebrate the recent Allied victory at El Alamein and the invasion of North Africa).

On November 17 she was OK'd by Dr Borthwick at White Waltham for light work, such as the Fairchild, until her injured hand was completely healed. November 20: 'My first time in air since my accident - wasn't least bit concerned and enjoyed myself as much as ever.'

On January 23, 1943, Ann was back at White Waltham, staying at Woolley Grange, and being trained to fly Class 3 (light twin-engined types like the Anson, Oxford and Dominie) with Joan Hughes as her instructor. January 28: 'Am thoroughly convinced White Waltham is a mad house and a terrific place to do training.' February 1: 'The entire school was given a free day as the drome is US (unserviceable) after yesterday's gale and rains. Went to Maidenhead to buy some wings at Blackstones.' (L.J. Blackstone was the tailor on Chapel Arches, opposite the Rialto cinema).

Ann did an hour's solo at Aldermaston on February 3 and gorged on real butter and almost-white bread. Outside she saw the Red Cross doughnut truck with 'three nifty-looking gals. They have gala time driving about, filling the boys up with coffee and their wares. They live in a hotel in Newbury.'

Back at Ratcliffe, now qualified on Class 3, she flew her first Oxford from Castle Bromwich to Wroughton: 'An Oxford is a piece of cake, particularly in bad weather.' Her first Anson was to Bircham Newton and on February 16 it was her first Lysander from Bristol to Barnstaple. 'Didn't get off till 1pm, what with all the boys rechecking everything to see it was OK. At these out-of-the-way places, they always doubt that a woman can fly.'

On May 5 she did her first Dominie job to Bicester and on May 11 picked up her first Spitfire IA at Kirkbride. 'It was best thing I ever flew and wished I had done some recent aerobatics so that I could have flung it around with some degree of confidence.' She was back at White Waltham to begin her Class 4 conversion to heavy twin-engined aircraft. Training was usually on the Blenheim and Hudson. May 30: 'They have started to fly Wimpeys (Vickers Wellingtons) from White Waltham with men checking tyres after each landing. Yesterday they got away with six or seven punctures which is on the decline.' (The glass came from 'compost' spread on the airfield which was found to contain nails, screws, tin-openers and table knives and resulted in the airfield being closed for 11 days.)

After qualifying, Ann returned to Ratcliffe and flew her first Wimpey from Lichfield to Ossington on June 15. June 20 she calls her jackpot day with a Mustang, a Tiger Moth and a Blenheim. On June 28, the final day of her diary entries, she flew a Spitfire from Castle Bromwich to Cosford and then a Beaufighter from High Ercol to North Coates. 'Really loved it - they (the Beaufighters) fly themselves.'

*Ann's final flights for ATA were in a Mosquito and two Harvards at the end of October 1945. She remained in Great Britain and eventually became the assistant to America's first civil air attache at the United States Embassy in London.*

*On her return to America she spent 12 years as director of public relations for Northeast Airlines; 12 years as staff vice-president, international airport charges, Pan American; and eight years as assistant to the chairman of Air New England. In 1996 she received the Godfrey L. Cabot Award for her lifetime achievements and contributions to aviation, and her pioneering efforts in opening opportunities in aviation to women through her efforts as a World War II pilot and in aviation management.*

# Appendix II

# 'I Only Want You To Do Ten Minutes'

ALAN DEERE, a New Zealander who took part in the Battle of Britain in 1940 as one of 'The Few' and also in the fighter operations over Dunkirk at the time of the evacuation of British troops, began his training as a pilot at White Waltham. He was in continuous action from the outbreak of war until 1943. He destroyed 22 enemy aircraft, damaged 18 and had ten probables (probably destroyed) credited to him. He sailed from New Zealand to Britain in September 1937 with 11 other New Zealanders who had been selected for training with the Royal Air Force. On the morning after arrival, the 12 reported to the New Zealand High Commissioner, Mr W.J. Jordan. Alan Deere, often known as Al Deere, left the RAF as an Air Commodore in 1967. He died in 1995, aged 77. The following extract comes from his autobiography, *Nine Lives*, originally published by Hodder and Stoughton in 1959 and later republished by Wingham Press.

AL DEERE, photographed as a Wing Commander in 1944. Photograph courtesy of the Imperial War Museum, London. Negative No CH13619

THE De Havilland Civil (sic) School of Flying at White Waltham near Maidenhead was to be our home for the next three months while we underwent an ab initio flying course before being finally accepted into the Royal Air Force as suitable for pilot training. A house called Altmore. whose postal address of Cherry Garden Lane never ceased to intrigue me, served as a mess for the pilot trainees, and it was here we arrived that same evening.

Our ship had been late and the start of the course had been delayed two days to enable us to be there on the opening day. This may have been the cause of the awkward silence which greeted us as we entered the ante-room to be met by the enquiring gaze of those who were to be our companions for the next three months. The looks we got suggested that it was all our fault, and what queer looking fish we were anyhow.

I wondered if they expected us to be black. After all, our national rugby side was known as the All Blacks and an English schoolboy was reputed to have written to his parents, after watching the All Blacks training on Eastbourne College grounds, that they seemed very nice and were almost white! Whatever the cause, there was not the enthusiastic reception which we had expected, as would have been the case in our own country under similar circumstances. Besides, and this rankled, the wretches had taken all the good rooms and left the only big room for us to be used as a dormitory...

It was to be some two weeks before I commenced flying. On my arrival, a pre-flying medical revealed that I had slight blood pressure and I was packed off to Halton (RAF Hospital) for observation, much to my chagrin. Repeated assurances that I felt one hundred per cent, had never had blood pressure in my life and that it was probably due to excitement, did not release me from kicking my heels around the Halton wards while my friends got on with their flying, some even going solo in that time. Eventually, sanity prevailed and I returned to White Waltham, determined to make good the ground that I had lost.

It was heartening to find that I had an instructor who fully understood how I felt and, as a result, made every effort to give me extra flying whenever possible, so that in the end I made up the lost ground. It was particularly unfortunate therefore that I should have angered this self-same instructor by disobeying instructions on my first solo, even though it was only through over-keenness. Having done the customary dual circuit prior to being sent solo, Flying Officer Dixon taxied the Tiger Moth to the downwind side of the airfield where he got out to give me final instructions before letting me take the aircraft solo for the first time.

'Remember your height and turning points on the circuit and make sure you are nicely settled down on the final glide in before choosing your spot to land. If you are in doubt don't be afraid to go round again and have no hesitation in doing so if you bounce badly on touch down. I only want you to do ten minutes and in that time you should be able to get in two landings.'

I was really straining at the leash by the time he had delivered these homilies and thinking he had finished, banged the throttle open - he always said I gave it a straight left - and so into the air, solo at last. One, two, three landings, around again and again I went, the ten-minute limit completely forgotten in the thrill and excitement of this momentous occasion. Finally, having convinced myself I was just about the best pupil that had ever flown a Tiger Moth, I taxied back to the airfield boundary, purring with pleasure.

'I thought I told you to make only two landings and not to take longer than ten minutes,' an infuriated instructor, his rather large moustache waxed solid with the cold, greeted me on my return. Somewhat deflated, I answered: 'Sorry, sir, I thought I was to go on until I was satisfied that the landing was perfect.'

'If that was the case, you would be up there for a week,' was the sarcastic reply. 'Not only did you disobey my instructions, you didn't even have the decency to wait until I had finished speaking, before opening the throttle and bloody nearly blowing me out of the field with the slipstream.'

Not a happy first solo. However, Flying Officer Dixon was not the one to nurse a grievance and, in fact, never mentioned the incident again. This says a lot for his patience, because it wasn't the only occasion on which I put his powers of self-control to the test.

*After two weeks officer training at RAF Station Uxbridge, Al Deere was posted to No 6 Flying Training School at Netheravon in Wiltshire. In his junior term there, he flew Hawker Harts.*

# Appendix III

# Life As A Ferry Pilot For The RAF

IN his research at the Public Record Office, the author discovered an article, prepared for publicity purposes in the offices of BOAC (British Overseas Airways Corporation) who were responsible for the administration of ATA. Accompanying it is a letter to the Ministry of Information, dated July 30, 1940, and signed by Kenneth Adam, suggesting the article should be used with the name of Joan Hughes as author. Whether the article was ever issued to newspapers or magazines is not known. Joan Hughes, then 22, had gained her wings at the age of 17 and was then the youngest woman pilot in the country. She was one of the first eight women to join ATA in January 1940 and one of the 11 women who qualified to fly four-engined aircraft. Joan served as an instructor in ATA and postwar was chief flying instructor at the West London Aero Club. She died in 1993, aged 74. The article describes a day in the life of an ATA pilot. As was usual at that time, for security reasons, no place names are given.

THE first thing I would like to make clear is that we

*JOAN HUGHES in the cockpit of a Short Stirling bomber. Photograph courtesy of the Imperial War Museum, London. Negative No HU90022.*

women members of the Air Transport Auxiliary do not regard ourselves as 'heroines.' We are doing what we hope is a useful job of work, but there is nothing spectacular about it, because we are, all twenty of us, thoroughly used to flying, and we think no more of piloting an aeroplane than we do of driving a car. That is not conceit; it is a plain statement of fact. Because, you see, most of us, before the war came along, were earning our living in civil aviation, as pilots or instructors. I was an instructor myself, at an aerodrome near London. I learned to fly when I was 17 - that is, five years ago - and when I was accepted last winter as one of the eight who made up the original women's unit, I had done about 600 hours solo. The qualification for a ferry pilot was 250 hours. Most of my colleagues - I was the youngest of them - had between 1000 and 2000 hours to their credit.

Perhaps the best way to give you an idea of our work is to describe a typical day's programme. We are attached to an aerodrome not very far from London and we report for duty each morning soon after nine o'clock. Some of us live in a hotel near the aerodrome; others in London or in our homes on the outskirts. By the time we arrive our chief, Pauline Gower, is very busy arranging the day's schedule. She is one of the most experienced air women in the country and has run our section of ATA most successfully

THE Percival Mew Gull in which Alex Henshaw set a new record for England to Cape Town and back in February 1939. Joan Hughes is seen in the Mew Gull after she had test flown it following a rebuild at White Waltham in the early 1950s.

since the beginning. She has to ring up, or is rung up by, various contractors all over the country. They report that they have certain aircraft waiting to be 'picked up' and taken to RAF maintenance units or training squadrons. The contractor may be in the south of England, the aircraft's destination is very likely to be 'somewhere in Scotland.' Or the factory may be in the north and the RAF station in the west.

In either case a journey of several hundred miles is involved, and now that production is being accelerated so greatly, the demands made on the four ferry pools - ours and the three staffed by men pilots - are growing every week, every day almost. When the preliminary list is complete - it will probably be added to in the course of the day - our Ferry Officer has to get a second list, because the girls have got to get to the factories as quickly as possible, and, very often, brought back by air to headquarters as well when they have delivered their aircraft. Sometimes, of course, they can do another delivery on the way back. Even so, a 'taxi' as we call these intermediate machines which carry the ferry-pilots about, have got to pick them up at 'X' and take them on to 'Y', where they will pick up their aircraft and go to 'Z'. So you will understand the schedule of the day's flights, when it is complete, will, on a busy day, and that really means every day on which flying is possible at all, be an extremely complicated one.

Well, all these arrangements are the business of the senior officers; meantime the rest of us sit and wait our call. There's a good deal of competition for our few comfortable chairs. The unlucky ones perch where they can, on a table or somewhere - there's no luxury about our 'rest-room' to put it mildly. We smoke and talk and knit - we've done quite a lot of knitting in such spare time as we do get - until the moment comes for us to go and get our 'chits.' Our uniform, by the way, is rather a smart one; I'm sure the girls in the WAAF are jealous of us. Theirs isn't nearly so nice. It has been adapted from the uniform which the pilots of British Airways used to wear. It's dark blue, and on the breast there are tiny gold wings with the letters 'ATA' worked into the middle. First officers have three gold bars on the shoulder, second officers two. Oh, and we girls wear skirts, not trousers. Pauline Gower thinks that even if women are doing a man's job of work that's no reason why they shouldn't continue to look feminine. Of course, when we're actually flying we have to wear regulation flying suits and parachutes rather like bustles at the back. And I don't think anybody would claim that all the very necessary paraphernalia improves our beauty! All the same, when we're not actually in the air, we do pride ourselves on our appearance! (Author's note: Trousers were also issued to the pilots and, as Lettice Curtis records in *The Forgotten Pilots*, were only meant to be worn on aerodromes)

Once we have been given our 'chits' we lose no time in getting away. These 'chits' are simply delivery and receipt slips - one which we leave with the contractor, and another which we bring back to headquarters signed by the officer in charge of the RAF aerodrome to which we have delivered the aircraft.

Several of us will pile into one 'taxi' - generally a Puss Moth - and very soon we're in the air on the way to the nearest factory where one of our number is to 'collect.' You probably wonder what it feels like to fly alone in wartime? Well, of course, there is always the bare chance that one may come across an enemy, and that does tend to keep one on the watch all the time! But happily the sky is a very large place and the chances of coming across a Dornier or a Messerschmitt are very small - especially as the RAF keep such a good look-out for such visitors. Anyway, we've had no excitement of that kind so far, in fact we are not a little proud that we have ferried several hundred aeroplanes so far without any trouble and strictly according to routine.

Mind you, there are certain complications about flying in wartime. We have to keep away from prohibited areas, where there are balloon barrages and other devices intended to... well, shall I say, make flying more difficult? We have to fly in all weathers, without the usual aid to navigation - meteorological reports, and so on, and at the best possible speed of which our aircraft are capable. No dawdling in the sky! And when we get to our destination we have to take certain steps to make sure that we are recognised as a friend before we touch down. (Author's note: Although no weather information was available in the air, as the pilots had no radio contact with the ground, weather information was available before take-off).

The Air Ministry is paying us a high compliment by asking us - both men and women in the ATA - to take on more work. In September last Mr Gerard d'Erlanger, with the encouragement of the Director-General of Civil Aviation, Sir Francis Shelmerdine, formed a pool of 33 ferry pilots - all men - who were attached to two RAF stations. That was the beginning of ATA. We women were recruited in December. There were only a handful of us in those days, Pauline Gower, who was taught to fly by Amy Johnson, of England-to-Australia fame, and afterwards joined an aerial circus, going into loops, spins and rolls every day between lunch and dinner; Winifred Crossley who had more than five years' experience in the air, including 'stunting'; Mona Friedlander, who was the first woman to do Army co-operation flying and is an ice-hockey international; the Hon Mrs Fairweather, eldest daughter of Lord Runciman, who used to be an inspector at Renfrew Airport for the Civil Air Guard before the war; Margaret Cunnison, another Scot, who won a bursary which enabled her to learn to fly and piloted one of the most beautiful pupils at the Scottish flying crews, Rosemary Rees, who has flown unconcernedly all over Europe in all sorts of weather by herself; Mrs Patterson whose corps of women pupils at Romford, near London, was quite famous last year; Mrs R. Wilberforce, who hails from Aberdeen - it's surprising how many Scotswomen seem to make good pilots - and myself, the 'baby' of the gang in those days.

Four of us had husbands in the forces, by the way. Well, since then we've grown considerably. Amy Johnson is one of those who've joined us. And it's not only in numbers that we have increased, but in duties. You see, early this year Mr d'Erlanger was asked to set up pools of his own, which should be run, not by the Royal Air Force but by himself and British Airways, one of whose wartime activities this is, and since February the number of machines which we carry every week in ATA has gone up 15 times. Before we used to ferry only from the factory to the RAF maintenance unit, because when an aircraft leaves a factory it still has to be fitted out inside, even though it can be flown. Now we ferry not only repaired aircraft but also fully equipped aircraft from the maintenance units to the various squadron headquarters themselves. At present we girls are flying elementary trainers, and advanced bomber-trainers and fighter-trainers, but we are hoping that very shortly we shall be handling Spitfires and Hurricanes and even big multi-engined bombers. I must say I'm looking forward to flying at 350 mph solo. No matter how long one has been flying, it's still a thrill to go faster.

Each girl undergoes what is called a 'conversion' course when she joins us. By the way, we call the newcomers

*From a later era - the Fairey Rotodyne (see page 67).*

'stooges' which is an American term of course, borrowed from the music-halls, and means the 'dumb partner' in an act, who gets all the kicks and is continually being made fun of by his clever partner. Actually, we are very fond of our 'stooges' and it is a term of affection really. They very soon get through their training and learn how to fly different types of aircraft. Of course, the bigger the machine, the more complicated the controls, and when you first come across the panel of an Anson or a Magister, after the simple dashboard of a Puss Moth, you think you've walked straight into a nightmare! However, all the various knobs and handles and wheels and clocks and gauges sort themselves out in time, and we get to know each panel more or less by heart. Our conversion courses have been taken at the Central Flying School of the RAF hitherto, but now the Training School belonging to British Airways has been pressed into service as well.

Well, there it is, that's our job and how we do it. It's very pleasant really in these summer days - much pleasanter, anyway, than when we were flying through the hardest winter Britain has had for 50 years and the bitter weather used to coat our wings with ice. We're hoping next winter won't be so severe, because, with the increased demand for pilots for strictly operational work, and the great acceleration of production under Lord Beaverbrook (Minister of Aircraft Production), we're expecting an even busier time ahead.

We are particularly gratified at the way in which the men pilots have accepted us as colleagues working on an equal footing. There's no society tea party atmosphere about this show of ours, and we are glad that the commander of ATA, Mr d'Erlanger, has been able to say of us, as he did the other day: 'The girls fly as neatly and precisely as the men.' That's the nicest compliment he could have paid to us, because neatness and precision are what are wanted in our job, not stunts or gallantry or anything like that. After all, when you're flying an aircraft worth a great many thousand pounds, you don't want to take any risks. 'Safety and punctuality' is our motto; we have lived up to it so far, and hope to go on doing so until the war is won, and we can feel that, in our own way, we have played our part.

*GROVE PARK, White Waltham, photographed in 2002. This was the site of the main part of the RAF camp. The Grove House (see page 58) can be clearly seen bottom right; the white-roofed building, the front of which can be seen on page 72, is on the old ML Aviation site. Photograph by courtesy of Michael Shanly Investments.*

# Appendix IV

# A Pilot to Remember

**BERT GOODCHILD, whose photograph appears on the cover of this book and on pages 20 and 22, died on March 14, 2005, aged 75. The following tribute was written by Tony Bianchi, managing director of Personal Plane Services Ltd, the company founded by his father, the late Doug Bianchi. Personal Plane Services is based at Wycombe Air Park, Booker, from where Bert often flew.**

ON March 14, 2005, British light aviation lost one of its most colourful characters and a highly versatile pilot. Bert, as he was universally known, was born in Henley-on-Thames in 1927 and lived most of his life in the White Waltham area. He was a passionate aviator with aeroplanes and all that goes with them firmly in his blood. His passion, above all, was for the Spitfire.

The entry in Bert's log book which records his first flight in a Spitfire on November 1, 1970. It lasted 20 minutes. Bert wrote at the top of the page: 'Flight to Remember? Ambition achieved'

Bert learned to fly whilst working for Fairey Aviation at White Waltham in 1948, gaining his licence on March 14, 1949. His instructor was Joan Hughes, the diminutive ferry pilot of ATA fame. Joan was a superb instructor and in Bert her talents showed their best. She said: 'He was a natural from the beginning.'

Once having gained his licence, Bert's sensible approach and capable hands soon inspired aeroplane owners to use him to ferry and flight

*continued on page 97*

Bert in a Spitfire Mark IA, flying over Stokenchurch, just north of Booker airfield, in the 1980s.

Bert and Doug Bianchi (right) in Hamburg in 1972. Bert flew this Fokker to promote the release of the film 'Zeppelin.' Over the years he flew many World War I aeroplanes in airshows and films and always had a sensitive feeling for these interesting types.

Ready to fly the 1912 Manning Flanders military monoplane at Booker in 1989.

With De Havilland Rapide G-AKIF at Booker in 1992. Bert was one of the most experienced Rapide pilots of his day.

Bert flying the 1927 Morane Saulnier 230, belonging to the Hon Patrick Lindsay.

The photo on Bert's aviator's certificate, issued on March 7, 1949, and signed by Lord Brabazon of Tara, president of the Royal Aero Club. Left, the certificate.

test their aeroplanes. Thus a huge amount of experience was rapidly gained on a multitude of different types, both single and multi-engine, in a relatively short time.

In the early 50s, Bert joined Personal Plane Services. Here he put his skills to best advantage, ferrying all sorts of aeroplanes to and from Europe. He was also responsible for a great deal of test flying and development flying on some of the new types introduced for production in the 50s and 60s. Most needed demonstrating, so Bert's air show flying began. He was an accomplished aerobatic pilot and always flew within his limits. He was usually the preferred pilot to get the job done and get the aeroplane back in one piece.

Bert flew on a number of film productions and TV commercials. In the type of flying he did, there were many occasions when problems occurred. Bert took these in a typically professional way and, with his excellent natural skills, he usually saved the day!

In the subsequent 40 years, Bert flew over 5000 hours in nearly 300 types of aircraft in addition to his main duties as ground crew and aircraft refuelling. Pilots visiting Booker in later years did not realise that this happy modest man had a long and exemplary background as a pilot, and was always willing to impart his great depth of aviation knowledge to others.

In 1970, Bert achieved his life's ambition and flew Adrian Swire's Mark IX Spitfire. Those who watched that day saw a man who truly deserved to fly precious aeroplanes, especially the Spitfire. In the ensuing years, Bert had many happy hours flying the PPS-operated Spitfires.

He always flew with great skill and sensitivity and absolutely by the book. Bert was simply the ideal Spitfire pilot! Seeing him deliver a Spitfire to Biggin Hill for the Air Fair, wearing his old leather helmet, PPS overalls and with a copy of The Sun stuffed in his pocket, took away the nonsense and brought reality to this kind of flying. Bert just got on with the job he loved - flying the aeroplane properly. He will be greatly missed by all who knew him.

# Appendix V

# We Never Fired in Anger

**WALTER (Wally) HEADINGTON, an airframe and engine fitter with ATA from 1941 to 1945, was a member of the anti-aircraft unit which formed part of the ATA Home Guard platoon on White Waltham airfield. They used twin Lewis guns, mounted on a tripod. But, as he explains in these reminiscences, the guns were never fired in anger.**

I first joined the Home Guard (then known as the Local Defence Volunteers) at Holyport in 1940. We all thought this was a good idea and would put us in good stead when we joined the proper Army. I transferred to the ATA Home Guard towards the end of 1942-43, but cannot remember the exact date.

Our duties at White Waltham airfield were to patrol the western perimeter at night from the main gate to the southern side of the RAF camp. During the day, if there was a 'red alert' (a warning that enemy aircraft were fairly near) we would man the two Lewis gun positions.

These guns were never fired in anger. Our orders were to 'only open fire if the enemy aircraft is attacking your position.' Otherwise, permission had to be obtained from the Territorial Army headquarters in Maidenhead - by which time the enemy aircraft would be back over the English Channel. The reasoning behind this order was that if you fired and missed, you gave away a gun position for no practical result. The aircraft would have had to be flying fairly low to be hit by a Lewis gun.

On night patrols we had a good view of the Dorney Common heavy anti-aircraft guns in action and could see the flashes of the shells exploding around that area. One thing I can remember of those patrols was being soaked if it was raining and being bitterly cold if it was a clear moonlit and frosty night. I didn't see anything of interest except the ghostly outlines of the aircraft parked at dispersal. One night we thought we saw a fox. (A treat!)

I think our Home Guard duties occurred every eighth night but every Wednesday from 1500 hours we were allowed to leave our work benches for infantry training, sometimes by a sergeant from the Grenadier Guards at Windsor (Wow!)

We did live firing on the rifle range at the rear of the hangars. The range had been built for the RAF flying pupils when the airfield was No 13 EFTS. We once did an exercise for a film unit - cannot remember its name. We loaded two Anson aircraft with Home Guard personnel and flew them from White Waltham to Forty Acres, the emergency landing ground at Waltham St Lawrence opposite what later became Wood's Yard. After we landed, we had to adopt a defensive position round the two aircraft and then charge towards a small copse. We

THIS photograph, taken at the airfield in January 1944, is of part of the ATA Home Guard unit, some of whom served in the anti-aircraft section. The two men standing furthest from the camera are unidentified. Those who can be named are: back row, fourth from left, Mr Tipple (first name not known); fifth from left, Ron Salmon; extreme right, Peter Hall; next to him, Bert Davis. Front row, extreme left, Corporal Wally Headington; next to him, Corporal Thomas; centre, Company Sergeant-Major Herbert Waite; extreme right, unknown; Sergeant Bert Fisher; Sergeant Batho; 2nd Lieutenant Ashplant; Lieutenant Spice. Others who served in the unit but are not in this photograph include Charlie Gorrod, Harry Spence, Maurice Hutt, Tom Sammons and Reed Herbert.

had a lorry to take us back to White Waltham as the field was not large enough for a fully loaded Anson to take off. Regrettably, I never saw the film.

On another occasion, when I was not on duty, I was told that just as dawn broke a Heinkel 111 was seen approaching the airfield from the direction of Maidenhead. It was flying very low, with one engine smoking badly. It flew across the airfield and turned south just before Shottesbrooke Church and disappeared into the early morning gloom. It was assumed to have been hit by Ack-Ack (anti-aircraft guns - not our Lewis guns) and was tree-topping back to base.

### BATTLE OF BRITAIN PARADE

DATED September 17, 1943, this photograph was taken on White Waltham airfield and is of a ceremony commemorating the Battle of Britain. The ATA Home Guard unit are on the left of the picture. The three aircraft which can be clearly seen are, left to right: a Fairchild Argus, a Lockheed Hudson and a Vickers Wellington. The minister conducting the service is almost certainly the Vicar of White Waltham, the Rev John Henry Jackson. Battle of Britain Day was September 15 - the day in 1940 when most German aircraft were shot down in the Battle. A ceremony was held in Kidwells Park in Maidenhead to mark the occasion. Members of the ATA Home Guard unit took part and Maidenhead Salvation Army Band played.

Elsewhere, a Battle of Britain parade was held in London in September 1943, in which ATA personnel took part. There were also parades at Coastal Command Headquarters at Northwood, Middlesex, and at Fighter Command Headquarters at Bentley Priory, Stanmore, also in Middlesex, on September 15 - the anniversary day.

When the Halifax bomber landed on the railway line (see page 47), the Home Guard was called out to keep people away as there was a bomb on board and live ammunition exploding. I helped to run a mains water fire hose from the main gate to the stricken aircraft as the first idea was to cool the bomb and keep the flames away while the ATA extracted the injured crew. By the time we had run out all these hoses, all the injured had been removed and we then beat a hasty retreat until the bomb exploded.

I was called up into the RAF so I don't know how the ATA Home Guard unit ended. I assume it was disbanded in late 1945.

## TEST BAY TEAM

GROUND staff played an essential role in maintaining and repairing the aircraft flown by ATA (see pages 6-10). These two photographs show members of the test bay team. They worked outside the hangar but were responsible for doing the final safety checks on aircraft which had been worked on by the hangar staff. These included the taxi aircraft which delivered ATA pilots to their assignments and, if necessary, collected them afterwards. They also dealt with any visiting aircraft and any which were due to be ferried elsewhere from White Waltham. The test bay team, which had been hand-picked by Wally Ludman, the engineer in charge, made the final checks before the planes were test flown. Members of the team were encouraged to go up on test flights with the pilot - a sure case of putting their money where their mouth was.

Main picture, back row, left to right: Wally Ludman (in charge); Ted (?) Roberts. odd-job man; Wally Whatmore, engine fitter; John Tomlinson, engine fitter (the author's brother). Front row, left to right, Jack Page, airframe fitter; Bob Powell, engine fitter; Bert Crosthwaite, engine fitter. Bert Crosthwaite ran the Bird in Hand pub at Knowl Hill. Small picture, left to right, Ken Golding, aiframe fitter; John Tomlinson, Ron Chapman, airframe fitter. They are standing in front of an Avro Anson.

# PRISONERS AT THE PRECAST

One other piece of undiscovered history has come to light since the third edition of this book was published. There was a small camp for German prisoners-of-war in White Waltham at the top of Butchers Lane, opposite what were the council houses. Some prisoners worked on local farms. They sometimes went to tea with local residents and Ken Ewers remembers that one or two of them made rocking-horses for local children.

Four prisoners were billeted at the Waltham Precast Concrete Company's Works at Woodlands Park and lived on the site. Mrs Sheila Collicutt, a granddaughter of the late Harry Wagner who owned the Precast, as it was known, has supplied the plan on page 103 and the photographs below. One of the prisoners, Heinz, then living in the Russian zone of Berlin, wrote to Mr Wagner in 1949 saying that his 14 months at the Precast were the happiest of his time as a prisoner.

Mrs Collicutt recalls that the prisoners made her a big wooden rocking-duck that she could sit in and a rocking-horse for her cousin. Her grandfather was also a building contractor and built many local houses and bungalows. He served on Cookham Rural District Council and provided the first building, in Smithfield Road, for Woodlands Park British Legion Club. He retired to Bampton, Oxfordshire, in 1952 and died in 1965. Her father, Bill Wagner, one of Harry's two sons, died in 1966.

The photos show: below, left, the sign for Cleveland, a pre and postwar petrol brand, and the red and white telephone box outside the works. The two Cleveland petrol pumps on site were operated by Hammants Garage, situated at Woodlands Park Corner. Below right, Harry Wagner. Bottom, left, the four German prisoners - foreground is Heinz. Bottom, right, Waltham Precast Company's works.

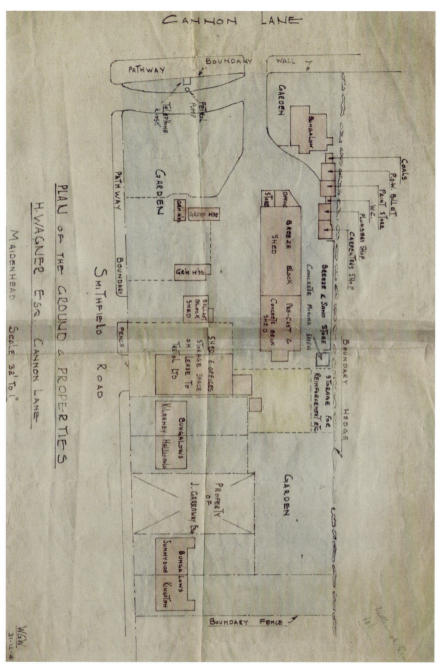

Detailed plan of Waltham Precast Concrete Company's works and adjoining properties in 1946. It was drawn by Walter (Wally) Wagner, Harry's other son. The prisoners' billet is clearly marked. Part of the site, on which six houses now stand, is named Wagner Close.

Copyright Maidenhead Advertiser

## ATA REMEMBERED

UNVEILING of the memorial plaque to Air Transport Auxiliary which took place at White Waltham airfield in June 2005. The plaque is sited outside the West London Aero Club clubhouse. The inscription on the memorial reads as follows:

## Air Transport Auxiliary
## 1939 - 1945

White Waltham was home to the Headquarters of the ATA and to No. 1 Ferry Pool, the Advance Flying Training School, the Communications Flight and the Engineering Training School. The ATA remained at White Waltham until the end of 1945 when it was disbanded.

Pilots from the ATA made over 308,000 deliveries of 147 different types of aircraft including Spitfires, Hurricanes, Ansons, Lancasters and Meteors. 173 men and women of the ATA, representing many nations, gave their lives during the World War of 1939-1945.

The plaque was unveiled by the Association's Commodore, Diana Barnato Walker, who flew with ATA from 1941-45 and piloted 82 different types of aircraft. In the photograph, left to right, are: Wing Commander Eric Viles, chairman of the Association; Diana Barnato Walker, Commodore of the Association; Peter George, a committee member who, as an ATA pilot, delivered 870 aircraft between 1941 and 1945 and spent numerous hours flying taxi aircraft which delivered the pilots to their assignments or collected them afterwards; Paul Jarvis, director of the British Airways Museum.

## THE OLD BARN

THIS photograph shows the former barn, situated next to St Mary's Church, White Waltham, which was used as a voluntary canteen for the forces during World War II (see page 59). The barn was converted to two houses in 1979. The one nearer the road is The Old Barn and the house at the rear is named Bryher Cottage. Built in 1749, the building was used as a tithe barn and was converted to a stable for the nearby Bury Court Farm in the early 1900s. The hayrack used by the horses was still in position during the war.

## PAST GLORY

THIS rare photo is of the mansion which once stood in Heywood Park (now Woodlands Park). The house, usually known as Heywood Manor, was demolished in the 1920s and the land surrounding it began to be developed for housing. Although the mansion was demolished, two buildings remained. One was a wing in red brick and housed the kitchen. The other was a two-storey yellow brick building which had been the coach house and stable block. It had living accommodation on the first floor. These were rooms known as bothies in which young men working on the estate, particularly in the gardens or in the stables, lived. This building was used during World War II as ATA's Engineering School and, after the war, housed WAAFs stationed at White Waltham. In January 1961, the building was used as an annexe for infants from White Waltham School and later became the temporary home for the whole school while building work was being carried out. This continued until July 1962 when the alterations to White Waltham School were completed and Woodlands Park School opened. The Lodge, on Waltham Road, which was the entrance lodge to the mansion site, is one of the two remaining links with this historic part of the neighbourhood. The other is Sawyers Crescent - named after the family who owned the Manor in the 19th and early 20th centuries. The name of the area was changed to Woodlands Park in the mid-1930s following two murders and a suicide. The bad publicity resulting from these tragedies was making it difficult to sell the new houses that were being built there and the change was made to help overcome this.